The Little Book of Big Sandwiches

The Little Book of Big Sandwiches

by Michael McLaughlin

illustrations by m.k.Mabry

CHRONICLE BOOKS

SAN FRANCISCO

Library of Congress Cataloging-in-Publication Data available.

ISBN 0-8118-0719-3

Printed in the United States of America.

Distributed in Canada
by Raincoast Books
8680 Cambie Street
Vancouver, B.C. V6P 6M9

10 9 8 7 6 5 4 3 2 1

Chronicle Books
275 Fifth Street
San Francisco, CA 94103

To Michael Honstein,

for friendship, computer advice,

and the guinea grinder

"Our family has combined the last two elements of protected hearthside and touristic nostalgia to invent a Railroad Sandwich which, we feel with smug modesty, is perfection. The recipe would be almost scandalous to print in proper form, involving as it does certain elements of live human flesh, but I can sketch a commendable outline, I hope. For one Railroad Sandwich, always referred to by its full name with some reverence, buy a loaf of the best procurable 'French' bread at least eighteen inches long to serve perhaps six people. Have on hand at least half a pound of sweet butter, not too cold to spread, and an equally generous pound or so of the highest quality sliced boiled ham. A pot of mustard of the Dijon type is indicated to add an optional fillip. Slice the loaf from end to end in two solid pieces, and then carefully remove all you can of the inner crumbs. All! Spread the two hollow shells generously with butter, and with judicious smears of mustard if desired. Lay upon the lower half of the loaf plenty of ham slices, overlapping thickly. Tuck them in a little at the edges, but not too neatly: a fringe is picturesque to some people, and pleasantly reminiscent; to my family it is essential. Put the two halves firmly together, and wrap them loosely in plastic or foil or wax paper, and then a clean towel. Then, and this is the Secret Ingredient, call upon a serene onlooker (a broad or at least positive beam adds to the quick results, and here I do not refer to a facial grimace but to what in other dialects is called a behind-*derrière*-bum-ass-seat-etc.), to sit gently but firmly upon this loaf for at least twenty minutes. One of the best of our sitters over some twenty years of assistance was Bonnie Prince Charlie Newton, built like a blade of grass during those useful and fargone years, but with a curiously potent electricity between his little beam and the loaf, almost like infrared cookery. He could make the noble sandwich flat without squirming on it, and melt the butter and marry it to the mustard and the crisp shattered crusts, better than anybody. Even without this charmer, though, a Railroad can be a fine thing, cut upon rescue into thick oblique slices and given the esoteric ingredients:

first a long loaf of French bread, then . . . then . . .”

M.F.K. Fisher
With Bold Knife and Fork

Table of Contents

The Serious Sandwich

Sandwiches deserve to be taken seriously, although not excessively so. From hamburgers to triple-decker clubs and from PB&Js to the sloppiest of sloppy joes, sandwiches are loved and devoured, especially by Americans, who like their food on the casual side. That is the basic appeal of the sandwich, I guess, that and the tactile involvement needed to get it to the mouth, and then the assorted textural pleasures, and the contrastable ones, too, with every mouthful holding a variety of good things, layered. Like a lot of other foods we enjoy for their speed and lack of pretense, sandwiches don't always get the respect they should. Something so basic and so improvisational hardly seems to need planning (much less a recipe), and talk of sandwich balance and technique and timing can sound all too much like making a plain thing complicated.

And yet, there are sandwiches, and then there are sandwiches, and although a slab of cold meat loaf slapped between two slices of white bread and eaten by the midnight light of the refrigerator may sometimes be just the culinary ticket (trust me, on this I'm an expert), other occasions and other hungers call for more substantial and inventive fare. While the best sandwiches should always be as casual to prepare as they are to eat, it is possible, with a little care and planning, to make a sandwich bordering on the sublime, a sandwich worth cooking up and serving to guests, a sandwich that is a star, not a snack. Such sandwiches are serious sandwiches, and as far as I am concerned, they are also big sandwiches: It is impossible to take three slices of cucumber between two pieces of thin white bread seriously.

Sandwiches made their impact on me early and often. The kids next door, of preschool age, as was I, happily ate baked-bean sandwiches while wandering around the yard shoeless and in overalls with one strap hanging. When I asked my mother for baked-bean sandwiches, she only smiled, knowing then, as I know now, that it was probably poverty that inspired those drippy snacks. So why do I still feel cheated?

I remember Bible-school-picnic paper-bag sandwiches—bologna ground with gherkins and moistened with Miracle Whip, on white bread with iceberg lettuce—sweet-salty and soggy, very sixties. There was a dessert sandwich, too, of chocolate frosting thickly spread between two squares of graham cracker. It was especially fine the next morning for breakfast, when the frosting had softened the crackers slightly, washed down with a glass of milk.

In Disneyland, once, at the underground Blue Grotto restaurant, just off the Pirates of the Caribbean ride, I was served a Monte Cristo dusted with powdered sugar and accompanied with both a jigger of currant jelly and a pitcher of maple syrup. The combination was as unreal as the electronic fireflies winking way off in Walt's faux bayou. (Not all big sandwich memories are good memories.)

I remember the bambino, an Italian sausage patty sandwich on a bun that was a staple for years at a certain Boulder, Colorado, tavern. Another Boulder sandwich (still only an unsampled dream of mine) was the now politically incorrect guinea grinder—ground beef, pizza sauce, mozzarella, pickles, and onions, on a steamy, foil-wrapped sub loaf. A recipe for eggplant parmigiana once came to me with the advice to save a helping, to be fried up in olive oil the next day (flattened with a spatula during the process into a kind of crisp cake) and stuffed into a soft Italian loaf. At Ferdinando's Foccoceria, in the Carroll Gardens section of Brooklyn, they serve a lot of *vasteddi*—sandwiches of spleen and ricotta, baked on house-made flatbread. Why are so many of the best big sandwiches Italian in spirit, if not fact?

A popular Manhattan hangout, located in the heart of the theater district, serves (or served) cheeseburgers so good that for the nine months I worked there, four shifts a week, I never ate anything else. I dipped my burgers and the excellent steak fries into the restaurant's thick and tangy homemade Russian dressing. In a bad case of chic, the burgers were not listed on the menu but were always available, to those far enough into the know to ask.

These are the big sandwiches of the past, but there are fresh obsessions every day. Down the road from where I write this, at what its owners describe as a "sleazy cantina," there is a club sandwich. Filled with real roast turkey, bacon, tomatoes, and cheese, it is built not on bread but on three stacked flour tortillas, baked, quartered, and served hot and gooey. Elsewhere in town, a large portobello mushroom cap is grilled and tucked into a good bun, along with lettuce, tomatoes, and fresh mayo—a mushroom burger, hold the beef. The newest promotional recipe from the Hormel company, makers of Spam, is the Spamburger, a crisply sauteed patty of the wonderful pink stuff, stacked onto a bun with melted cheese, lettuce, tomato—not a replacement for the hamburger, but not a bad big sandwich. To get the historical big sandwich picture (I won't bore you with tales of the Earl of Sandwich, who surely didn't invent the food that bears his title) it's worth noting that the first trademark ever registered in this country (the year was 1867) was for William Underwood's canned deviled ham, a product that actually didn't achieve great success until Americans began brown bagging their lunches.

Eaten in pajamas or tux, leaning over the sink or sitting at a table, washed down by cold beer or good Champagne, serious sandwiches always begin with good bread. There's plenty of that around these days, even on supermarket aisles; the seriously deprived can even bake their own, and I have included a sensibly limited few in this book. Such premium breads are more than just a way to keep the mayo off your fingers. Crusty, grainy, full-flavored, sometimes with added flavor-makers like herbs, nuts, seeds, onions, garlic, or dried tomatoes, good bread is the foundation on which a serious big sandwich is built.

Since artisanal bakers spend so much time achieving the crusts of these handmade, hearth-baked breads, it seems a shame to trim them off, and so I don't. You will not find sandwiches in this book that are made on bagels, tortillas, croissants, English muffins, corn bread, scones, pancakes, waffles, or slabs of grilled polenta.

Nor do such nonbread-based finger foods as tacos, egg rolls, and burritos qualify, partly because I'm old-fashioned and partly because by intent this book is small, to avoid being enormous, which is the size book it would take to encompass all sandwich possibilities. If you don't mind how soggy English muffins get when topped with properly juicy burgers, or the way the tuna salad squirts out the hole in the bagel, by all means use 'em: Compulsive sandwich making is no fun at all.

Premium bread demands other topnotch ingredients, and while sandwiches and leftovers often go hand in hand, the best serious sandwiches are made on purpose, of fresh ingredients, resulting in succulent eating. Fresh mayonnaise (especially if and when the government and the egg industry get around to fixing the unforgivably long-lasting salmonella problem) is the best friend a sandwich ever had. Mayonnaise from a jar is by no means unacceptable; indeed, the quality and ease of access are perfect arguments for twisting that lid. (If you substitute lower-fat or reduced-cholesterol mayonnaise in the recipes in this book, you may want to add a few drops of lemon juice or a teaspoon of mustard to it to balance the flavor. For some reason these products are sweetened rather heavily.)

Finally, it is important to have a sense of history. Modern kitchen nomenclature, which often seems to be nothing more than a list of the major ingredients in the dish in question, has erroneously led some cooks to the belief that randomly chosen representatives of several food groups, smeared with mustard and trapped between two slices of bread, constitute a sandwich. While it's true that a certain amount of kitchen innovation keeps us on our toes, the best sandwiches are based on classic models and traditional combinations, favorites that have stood the test of time, big sandwiches that have been serious almost as long as Dagwood has been hungry.

American Style

Palm Beach Sandwiches
Roast Pork and Apple Sandwiches with Horseradish Mayonnaise

Madeira Roast Loin of Pork
Bratwurst-and-Kraut Melts

Chopped Chicken Salad Sandwiches with Tarragon and Walnuts
BLT and G(uacamole)

Barbecued Pork Tenderloin Sandwiches with "Burnt" Edges Slaw
Smoked Turkey Reubens

Proustian Sloppy Joes
Grilled Hamburgers with Sour Cream and Herbs

Cobb Sandwiches
New York Street Dogs

Palm Beach Sandwiches

makes 8 big sandwiches

Despite their genteel Floridian name, these Cheddar-cheese-and-red-pepper-salad-filled sandwiches are popular throughout the South and are particularly celebrated in El Paso, where they are a staple at The Women's Club Antique Show. Good cooks embellish them variously (substituting homemade red pepper conserve or diced green chiles for the roasted peppers, for example, or supplementing either with chopped pecans); hasty cooks don't hesitate to resort to jarred pimientos. At The Women's Club the bread crusts are trimmed; in this big sandwich book, they are not.

2   large, heavy red sweet peppers
¾   cup mayonnaise, fresh (page 89) or purchased
½   cup thinly sliced green onions
1   tablespoon fresh lemon juice
1   tablespoon Dijon mustard
¾   teaspoon hot pepper sauce
¾   pound sharp Cheddar cheese, coarsely grated
16 thick slices firm white sandwich bread

In the flame of a gas burner or under a preheated broiler, roast the peppers, turning them, until the skins are lightly and evenly charred. Slip the peppers into a paper bag, close the top and steam the peppers until cool. Rub away the burnt peel, then stem and core the peppers and finely chop them.

In a large bowl, stir together the chopped peppers, mayonnaise, green onions, lemon juice, mustard, and hot pepper sauce. Gradually stir in the grated cheese, mixing thoroughly. The sandwich filling can be prepared up to 1 day ahead. Cover and refrigerate; return it to room temperature before proceeding.

Up to 30 minutes before serving time, lay 8 slices of bread on a work surface. Divide the filling evenly among the slices, spreading it to the edges of the bread and using it all. Top with the remaining 8 slices of bread. With a serrated knife, carefully cut the sandwiches in half on the diagonal. Cover the sandwiches with plastic wrap and then drape them with a dampened towel until serving.

Roast Pork and Apple Sandwiches with Horseradish Mayonnaise

makes 4 big sandwiches

Sandwiches have a long history as the final resting place for assorted leftover meats, lubricated into some kind of edibility by plenty of mayo, mustard or whatever. The Dagwood spirit that pervades this book notwithstanding, such refrigerated improvisations may be frugal and filling, but rarely are they high kitchen art. For that you need a plan such as the following, which produces one of the most satisfying sandwiches I know. If you have no leftover roast pork, see my easy recipe, which follows. Watercress can be substituted for the radish sprouts.

⅔ cup prepared horseradish

⅔ cup mayonnaise, fresh (page 89) or purchased

4 Nice Buns (page 87) or any large, round good-quality sandwich rolls, split horizontally

1 pound roast pork loin, thinly sliced, at room temperature
Salt
Freshly ground black pepper

1 large, crisp sweet apple, such as Gala, halved, cored and thinly sliced

2 cups loosely packed radish sprouts

In a fine-mesh strainer, press the horseradish with the back of a spoon to extract the liquid. In a small bowl, stir together the drained horseradish and mayonnaise.

Spread the cut sides of the rolls with the mayonnaise mixture, dividing it evenly and spreading it to the edges. Arrange the pork slices in an overlapping layer on the bottoms of the rolls, dividing it evenly and using it all. Season the pork to taste with salt and pepper. Arrange the apple slices, spoke fashion, over the pork. Top the apples with the sprouts, dividing them evenly and using them all. Set the tops of the rolls in place. With a serrated knife, cut the sandwiches in half. Serve immediately.

Madeira Roast Loin of Pork

makes 2 pounds cooked meat

2   tablespoons loosely packed
     fresh thyme leaves
3   garlic cloves, crushed through a press
1   teaspoon salt
¾   teaspoon freshly ground black pepper
1   tablespoon olive oil
1   pork loin roast, about 2½ pounds,
     boned and tied, at room temperature
1   cup water
½   cup medium-dry (Sercial) Madeira wine

Position a rack in the middle of an oven and preheat to 350 degrees F.

In a small bowl, combine the thyme, garlic, salt, and pepper. With the back of a spoon, mash it all together into a rough paste. Stir in the olive oil.

Set the pork loin on a rack in a shallow roasting pan. Rub the pork with the thyme mixture. Roast for 30 minutes. Add the water to the roasting pan, baste the pork with ¼ cup of the Madeira, and roast for 10 minutes. Baste with the remaining ¼ cup Madeira and roast for 10 minutes. Continue roasting the pork, basting with the accumulated pan juices every 5 to 7 minutes, until an instant-read thermometer inserted into the center of the roast registers 160 degrees F, another 15 to 20 minutes.

Serve some of the pork hot, if desired, letting it rest on a cutting board, tented with foil, for 10 minutes before removing the strings and carving. Or, let it cool to room temperature. The roast can be prepared up to 2 days ahead. Wrap well and refrigerate; return it to room temperature before using.

Bratwurst-and-Kraut Melts

makes 6 big sandwiches

I first sampled these hearty (okay, rich) griddled sandwiches at
The Walnut Brewery, a brew pub in Boulder, Colorado. If all representatives of
this booming new restaurant category turn out product as fine as this one's gold
medal-winning Old Elk Brown Ale, things are indeed looking up for beer drinkers.
Sample a large glass of Old Elk the next time you're in Boulder; make the sandwich
(and wash it down with a glass of someone's good beer) ASAP.

1   pound fresh (not canned) sauerkraut, well drained
6   fully cooked bratwurst (about 1 pound total)
1   bottle (12 ounces) lager beer
2   tablespoons corn oil
12 large slices marbled pumpernickel-rye bread (see note)
1   cup honey mustard
¾   pound aged Gruyère or Swiss cheese, thinly sliced
6   tablespoons unsalted butter, at room temperature

Position a rack in the middle of an oven and preheat to 400 degrees F. Wrap the sauerkraut in a small packet of foil and heat it in the oven until steaming, about 20 minutes.

Meanwhile, in a large skillet, combine the bratwurst, beer, and corn oil. Set over medium heat and bring to a simmer. Cook, turning the bratwurst often, until the beer has evaporated and the bratwurst are glazed and lightly browned, about 15 minutes. Transfer the bratwurst to a board and cut them in half lengthwise.

Lay the bread slices on a work surface. Spread one side of each slice with some of the honey mustard, dividing it evenly and using it all. Lay 2 bratwurst halves over the mustard on 6 of the slices. Top the bratwurst with the hot sauerkraut, dividing it evenly and using it all. Lay the cheese slices over the sauerkraut, dividing them evenly and using them all. Invert the remaining 6 slices of bread, mustard side down, onto the cheese. Spread the tops of the sandwiches with half the butter, dividing it evenly.

Set 2 large skillets (or a large griddle) over medium heat. Lay the sandwiches, buttered side down, in the skillets. Cover and cook until the bottoms are crisp and brown, about 5 minutes. Spread the tops of the sandwiches evenly with the remaining butter, turn them, cover with a lid, and cook until the cheese has melted, the bottoms are crisp and brown, and the sandwiches are heated through, another 3 to 4 minutes.

Transfer to a cutting board. With a sharp knife, cut the sandwiches in half on the diagonal. Serve immediately.

Note: Marbled bread consists of two types of dough, usually pumpernickel and rye or white, twisted together before baking to create a marbled effect in slices of the finished product. Plain pumpernickel or rye can be substituted.

Chopped Chicken Salad Sandwiches with Tarragon and Walnuts

makes 6 big sandwiches

Gourmet carryout chicken salads, lavishly dressed and consisting of gigantic chunks of poached white meat, are grand food, but really meant to be enjoyed plated, not as sandwich fillings. For that purpose, I hark back to a simpler era, when chicken salads included dark as well as light meat and were rather finely chopped and modestly dressed--ideal between two slices of bread. Here is such a salad, embellished, I must admit, with tarragon and walnuts--gourmet carryout touches of the best kind.

1   chicken, about 4 pounds, quartered
1   medium-sized yellow onion, chopped
1   medium carrot, peeled and chopped
      About 3 quarts water
2½   teaspoons salt
1   teaspoon dried thyme, crumbled
2   bay leaves
1¼   cups mayonnaise, fresh (page 89)
      or purchased
2   tablespoons fresh lemon juice
2   teaspoons dried tarragon, crumbled
¾   teaspoon freshly ground black pepper
1   cup finely diced celery
½   cup coarsely chopped walnuts
12   slices firm white sandwich bread
2   ripe tomatoes, thinly sliced
6   leaves crisp lettuce, such as romaine

Place the chicken, onion, and carrot in a heavy-bottomed 5-quart pot. Add just enough water to cover the solids. Set over medium heat and stir in 2 teaspoons of the salt, the thyme, and bay leaves. Cover partially and bring slowly to a simmer. Cook gently, turning once, until the chicken is almost done, with just a touch of pink showing near the bone of the dark-meat quarters, about 15 minutes. Remove the pot from the heat and cool the chicken to room temperature in the poaching liquid.

Remove the chicken from the poaching liquid (reserve the broth for another use) and pat dry. Remove and discard the skin. Pull the meat from the bones. With a long knife, chop the meat into approximately ½-inch pieces.

In a large bowl, whisk together the mayonnaise, lemon juice, tarragon, pepper, and the remaining ½ teaspoon of salt and let stand at room temperature for 30 minutes. Stir in the chicken, celery, and walnuts; adjust the seasoning.

Up to 30 minutes before serving time, lay 6 slices of bread on the work surface. Divide the chicken mixture evenly among the slices, spreading it to the edges of the bread and using it all. Arrange the tomato slices and lettuce leaves atop the chicken mixture. Set the remaining slices of bread atop the lettuce. With a sharp knife, cut the sandwiches in half on the diagonal. Cover with plastic wrap and drape with a dampened towel until serving.

Variations: Dried basil can be substituted for the tarragon. The bread can be lightly toasted.

BLT and G(uacamole)

It's a simple trick, but replacing the mayo with a generous
schmear of guacamole turns the familiar bacon, lettuce and tomato sandwich into
something fresh and exciting. Serve it with three-bean salad
and drink a cold Mexican beer.

2   large, ripe Haas avocados (about 1 pound total), pitted and peeled
2   tablespoons minced fresh cilantro
2   pickled jalapeños, drained and minced
2   teaspoons fresh lime juice
¾   teaspoon salt
12 strips thick cut bacon (about 1 pound total)
8   slices Whole-Wheat Toasted Cornmeal Bread (page 88) or any light-textured whole-grain bread
1   large, ripe tomato, thinly sliced
4   leaves crisp lettuce, such as romaine

Preheat a broiler. In a medium bowl, mash the avocado. Stir in the cilantro, jalapeños, lime juice, and salt. Set the guacamole aside.

Lay the bacon strips in a large skillet. Set the skillet over medium heat and cook, turning the bacon once or twice, until the strips are crisp, about 8 minutes. Drain on paper towels.

Meanwhile, under the broiler, toast the bread slices lightly on one side only.

While the bread slices are still warm, spread the guacamole over the untoasted side of each slice, dividing it evenly and using it all. Divide the warm bacon strips over the guacamole on 4 pieces of bread. Top the bacon with the tomato slices. Top the tomato slices with the lettuce leaves. Set the remaining 4 slices of bread atop the lettuce, guacamole side down. With a sharp knife, cut the sandwiches in half on the diagonal. Serve immediately.

Barbecued Pork Tenderloin Sandwiches with "Burnt" Edges Slaw

makes 6 big sandwiches

Recalling (without duplicating) genuine Carolina barbecued pork sandwiches, these are nevertheless just as smoky, messy, and satisfying to eat. The edges and ends of the pork are not actually burnt, only deliciously glazed and crisp; they are stirred into the slaw that goes atop the sandwiches, leaving no succulent morsel uneaten.

½ cup hot, thick, smoky tomato-based barbecue sauce

½ cup orange marmalade

¼ cup hot pepper sauce

½ cup mayonnaise, fresh (page 89) or purchased

3 tablespoons Dijon mustard

¾ teaspoon sugar

4 cups finely shredded green cabbage

2 cups wood-smoking chips, preferably hickory

3 pork tenderloins, about 1 pound each, trimmed of fat

6 Nice Buns (page 87) or any large, round good-quality sandwich rolls, split horizontally

In a small bowl, stir together the barbecue sauce, marmalade, and hot pepper sauce. In a large bowl, whisk together the mayonnaise, ½ cup of the barbecue sauce mixture, the mustard, and sugar. Add the cabbage, stir to combine, and adjust the seasoning (the slaw should be spicy). Cover and refrigerate for up to 1 hour.

Soak the wood chips in water to cover for 30 minutes.

Meanwhile, light a charcoal fire and let it burn down until the coals are evenly white, or preheat a gas grill (medium).

Drain the wood chips and scatter them over the coals or firestones. Position the grill rack about 6 inches above the heat source. Lay the tenderloins on the rack, cover the grill, and cook for 4 minutes. Brush the tenderloins generously with some of the remaining barbecue sauce mixture, turn, and grill them, covered, for 4 minutes. Continue brushing the tenderloins and turning them every 2 minutes or so until they are well glazed and done (just lightly pink at the thickest part), about 18 minutes total.

Transfer the tenderloins to a cutting board. Trim off and coarsely chop the crisp brown edges and the tapering end of each tenderloin and stir the pieces into the slaw. With a sharp knife, thinly slice the tenderloins, cutting across the grain and at a slight angle. Pile the warm sliced pork on the bottoms of the buns, dividing it evenly and using it all. Generously top the pork on each bun with a mound of slaw and set the bun tops in place. With a serrated knife, cut the sandwiches in half. Serve immediately. Pass any remaining slaw at the table.

Smoked Turkey Reubens

makes 4 big sandwiches

The specifics of the original Reuben are in question. Was it made with corned beef, baked ham, or turkey? Did it include sauerkraut or coleslaw? Was it invented at Reuben's Delicatessen in New York or by a wholesale grocer in Omaha? Should it be hot or not? Such speculation is fun, so long as it doesn't divert us from actually cooking up and enjoying some version of this classic big sandwich. Here, I have used sliced smoked turkey breast, and my sandwich is griddled (what we used to call grilled), since I think the contrast between hot, crusty exterior and cool, crunchy interior is what makes any Reuben special.

½   cup Russian dressing
2   tablespoons honey mustard
2   tablespoons minced fresh dill
½   teaspoon freshly ground black pepper
¼   teaspoon salt
3   cups finely shredded green cabbage
8   thin slices seeded rye or pumpernickel bread
6   ounces Swiss cheese, thinly sliced
½   pound smoked turkey breast, thinly sliced
½   stick (4 tablespoons) unsalted butter, at room temperature

In a medium bowl, whisk together the Russian dressing, honey mustard, dill, pepper, and salt. Add the cabbage, toss well, and let the coleslaw stand at room temperature for 30 minutes.

Lay the slices of bread on a work surface. Top the bread slices with the cheese, dividing it evenly and folding or trimming it to fit if necessary. Arrange the turkey evenly over the cheese on 4 of the bread slices, dividing it evenly and folding or trimming it to fit if necessary. Top the turkey with the coleslaw, dividing it evenly and using it all. Set the remaining 4 slices of bread, cheese side down, atop the slaw. Spread the tops of the sandwiches with half of the butter, dividing it evenly.

Set a large skillet (or griddle) over medium heat. Lay the sandwiches, buttered side down, in the skillet. Cover and cook until the bottoms are crisp and browned, about 5 minutes. Spread the tops of the sandwiches evenly with the remaining butter, turn them, cover and cook until the cheese has melted, the bottoms are crisp and browned, and the sandwiches are heated through, another 3 to 4 minutes.

Transfer to a cutting board and, with a serrated knife, cut the sandwiches in half on the diagonal. Serve immediately.

Variation: For a classic Reuben, substitute thinly sliced corned beef for the turkey.

Proustian Sloppy Joes

makes 8 big sandwiches

Not quite the suppertime ones my mother made, these joes are designed to taste the way I <u>remember</u> Mom's (which is to say, bolder than the original thing), and when I lick my sweet-tangy and slightly greasy fingers after consuming one, I'm always transported back to childhood. This makes a lot of sandwiches, because feeding a crowd is one of the virtues of the sloppy joe; any leftover meat mixture can be frozen for a second, even easier meal.

3	tablespoons olive oil
1½	cups finely chopped yellow onions
1	tablespoon medium-hot pure (unblended) chile powder or imported hot paprika
1	teaspoon dried thyme, crumbled
2	pounds ground chuck
¾	cup beef broth
¾	cup bottled chili sauce, such as Heinz
1	can (10¾ ounces) condensed tomato soup
1	tablespoon Worcestershire sauce
1	teaspoon salt
½	teaspoon freshly ground black pepper
8	Nice Buns (page 87) or any large, round good-quality sandwich rolls, split horizontally and then toasted, if desired
½	pound coarsely grated sharp Cheddar cheese

In a large skillet over medium heat, warm the olive oil. Add the onions, cover, and cook, stirring once or twice, for 5 minutes. Add the chile powder and thyme, cover, and cook, stirring once or twice, for 5 minutes. Crumble the ground chuck into the skillet and cook, breaking up the lumps with the edge of a spoon, until the meat has lost its raw color, about 10 minutes. Stir in the beef broth, chili sauce, tomato soup, Worcestershire sauce, salt, and pepper and bring to a simmer.

Lower the heat slightly, cover partially, and cook, stirring often, until thick, about 30 minutes. The meat mixture can be prepared up to 3 days ahead. Cool to room temperature, cover, and refrigerate; return to a simmer over low heat before proceeding.

Set the bottoms of the buns on plates. Spoon about ⅔ cup of the meat mixture onto each bottom. Sprinkle the meat with the cheese, dividing it evenly and using it all. Set the tops of the buns in place and serve immediately.

Variation: Replace the chili sauce with purchased tomato-based hot salsa. Serve the meat mixture in crisp taco shells, topped with grated Cheddar cheese and shredded lettuce.

Grilled Hamburgers with Sour Cream and Herbs

makes 8 big sandwiches

A dry burger is a crime. A <u>big</u> dry burger is even worse. Avoid that transgression by using ground beef that is not too lean (chuck is ideal) and stir in a bit of sour cream--what Julia Child once called the "optional James Beard enrichment"--by way of moisture insurance. Plenty of fresh herbs and a garnish of smoky grilled onions complete the perfect burger.

2⅔ pounds ground chuck
¼   cup sour cream
1   tablespoon minced fresh thyme
1   tablespoon minced fresh flat-leaf parsley
1   teaspoon minced fresh rosemary
¾   teaspoon freshly ground black pepper
2   cups wood-smoking chips, preferably hickory
4   medium-sized red onions, trimmed, peeled and halved crosswise
3   tablespoons olive oil
    Salt
8   Nice Buns (page 87) or any large, round good-quality hamburger buns, split horizontally Ketchup, mustard, and mayonnaise for serving (optional)

In a medium bowl, using a fork, stir together the ground chuck, sour cream, thyme, parsley, rosemary, and pepper. Lightly form the meat into 8 equal patties 1 inch thick. Cover the patties with plastic wrap and refrigerate for 1 hour.

Soak the wood chips in water for 30 minutes. Meanwhile, light a charcoal fire and let it burn down until the coals are evenly white or preheat a gas grill (medium-high).

Drain the wood chips and scatter them over the firestones or coals. Position the grill rack about 6 inches above the heat source. Brush the onion slices evenly on both sides with the olive oil. When the wood chips are smoking heavily, lay the hamburger patties and the onion slices on the rack, cover, and cook for 4 minutes. Turn, cover, and cook for another 3 to 4 minutes for medium-rare beef; the onions should be well browned and just tender. Transfer the hamburger patties and the onion slices to a plate and season lightly with salt to taste. If desired, toast the buns on the grill, cut side down, until lightly browned, about 2 minutes.

Set the bottoms of the buns on plates. Place the hamburger patties on the bottoms, top each with a slice of grilled onion, and set the bun tops in place. Serve immediately, accompanied with ketchup, mustard and mayonnaise, if desired

Variation: Top each hamburger patty, about 2 minutes from when you estimate it will be done, with a slice of good-quality Cheddar cheese.

Cobb Sandwiches

makes 4 big sandwiches

The elegant twist on the traditional chef's salad named for Mr. Cobb (a gentleman otherwise without apparent renown) is a California classic, originally created, if memory serves, at that Hollywood institution, The Brown Derby. The same basic rundown of ingredients (cooked poultry, bacon, avocado, greens, blue-cheese dressing) also makes a delicious sandwich, a kind of cousin to the club. Hard-cooked eggs may sometimes appear in the salad, but not, I think, in the sandwich; enjoy one on the side.

12   strips bacon (about ¾ pound total)
8   slices firm white sandwich bread
½   cup chunky blue-cheese salad dressing
½   pound cooked turkey breast, thinly sliced
½   large, ripe Haas avocado, pitted, peeled, and cut into 12 slices
1   large, ripe tomato, cut into 8 thin slices
4   medium leaves crisp lettuce, such as romaine

Preheat a broiler. Meanwhile, lay the bacon strips in a large skillet. Set the skillet over medium heat and cook, turning the bacon once or twice, until the strips are crisp, about 8 minutes. Drain on paper towels. Toast the bread on one side only.

While the bread slices are still warm, spread the dressing to the edges of the untoasted side of each slice, dividing it evenly and using it all. Arrange the turkey over the dressing on 4 slices of the bread. Lay the avocado over the turkey. Lay the warm bacon strips over the avocado, dividing them evenly. Top the bacon with the tomato slices. Top the tomato slices with the lettuce leaves. Set the remaining 4 bread slices atop the lettuce, dressing side down, and press firmly with the palm of your hand to flatten slightly. With a sharp knife, cut the sandwiches in half on the diagonal and serve immediately.

New York Street Dogs

makes 8 big sandwiches

Democracy in Manhattan is at its most viable around the carts of street vendors who purvey well-garnished frankfurters under umbrellas bearing the Sabrett name. Secretaries and CEOs (or at least middle managers) alike, leaning forward slightly to prevent unsightly stains on the fronts of their power outfits, companionably inhale a Sabrett or two with the efficient haste that is the very essence of New Yawk. Piling on the optional free toppings can double the volume of what is already a very economical meal. Among the most unlikely but essential of these is an orangy-red onion concoction very much like the one below. Accompany the dogs with individual bags of Charles Chips, cans of soft drinks outfitted with straws, and plenty of cheap paper napkins.

3	tablespoons corn oil
4	cups chopped yellow onions
1	teaspoon ground turmeric
1	teaspoon whole yellow mustard seeds
1	can (8 ounces) tomato sauce
3	tablespoons red wine vinegar
2	tablespoons Worcestershire sauce
2	tablespoons packed golden brown sugar
4	teaspoons soy sauce
1	tablespoon molasses
8	frankfurters
8	frankfurter buns
	Sweet pickle relish and bright yellow mustard for serving (optional)

In a medium, nonreactive saucepan over low heat, warm the corn oil. Add the onions, turmeric, and mustard seeds; cover and cook, stirring occasionally, for 10 minutes. Stir in the tomato sauce, vinegar, Worcestershire sauce, sugar, soy sauce, and molasses. Bring to a simmer and cook uncovered, stirring often, until thick, about 20 minutes. Remove from the heat and let cool to room temperature; for the best flavor, cover and refrigerate overnight. The onion mixture can be prepared up to 3 days ahead.

Position a rack in the middle of an oven and preheat to 400 degrees F. In a small saucepan over low heat, rewarm the onion mixture until simmering. In a medium saucepan, cover the frankfurters with water. Place over low heat, bring the water to a simmer, and cook until the frankfurters are heated through, about 10 minutes.

Set the frankfurter buns directly on the oven rack and bake until heated through and slightly crisp, about 4 minutes.

Remove the frankfurters from the water and drain them briefly on paper towels. Place a frankfurter in each bun and serve immediately, accompanied with the onion mixture and the relish and mustard, if desired.

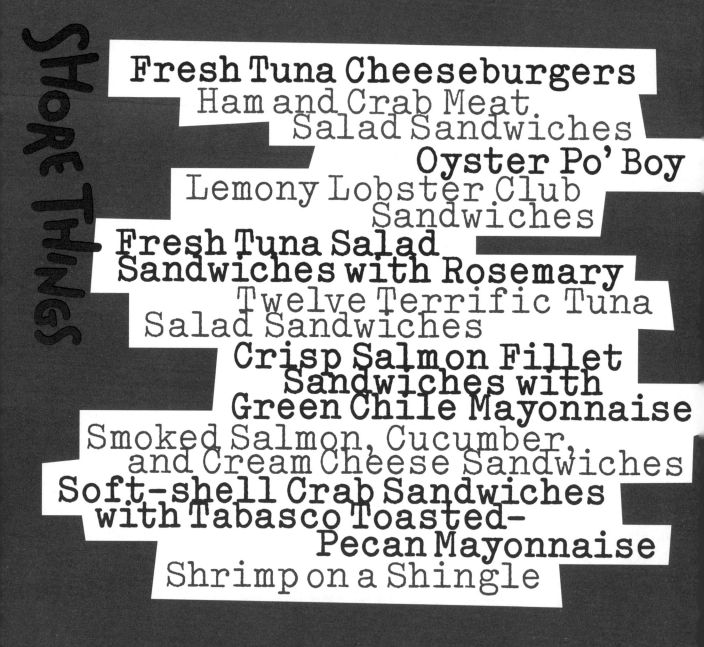

SHORE THINGS

Fresh Tuna Cheeseburgers

Ham and Crab Meat
Salad Sandwiches

Oyster Po' Boy

Lemony Lobster Club
Sandwiches

**Fresh Tuna Salad
Sandwiches with Rosemary**

Twelve Terrific Tuna
Salad Sandwiches

**Crisp Salmon Fillet
Sandwiches with
Green Chile Mayonnaise**

Smoked Salmon, Cucumber,
and Cream Cheese Sandwiches

**Soft-shell Crab Sandwiches
with Tabasco Toasted-
Pecan Mayonnaise**

Shrimp on a Shingle

Fresh Tuna Cheeseburgers

makes 2 big sandwiches

Using ground fresh tuna in place of tuna salad transforms the prosaic notion of the tuna melt (not to mention the cheeseburger) into an extraordinary eating experience. Shaped into generous patties and panfried until crisp on the outside, juicy pink within, the burgers are served on toasted buns, garnished with slices of tomato, leaves of crisp romaine, and mayonnaise.

1   pound fresh tuna fillet or steak, in one piece, well chilled
2   tablespoons mayonnaise, fresh (page 89) or purchased, plus additional mayonnaise for serving
1   tablespoon unsalted butter
1   tablespoon corn oil
     Salt
     Freshly ground black pepper
2   slices sharp American cheese
2   Nice Buns (page 87) or any large, round good-quality hamburger buns, split horizontally
4   medium slices ripe tomato
2   medium leaves crisp lettuce, such as romaine

Trim the tuna, removing any skin, bones (if using tuna steak) and the dark blood line that runs along the side. Cut the tuna into 1-inch chunks. In a food processor, using short bursts of power, chop the tuna. (Do not purée; some texture, like that of ground beef, should remain.) In a medium bowl, combine the tuna and the 2 tablespoons mayonnaise and mix lightly. Divide the tuna mixture in half; form each half into a patty about ¾ inch thick.

In a medium skillet over medium-high heat, melt together the butter and corn oil. Add the tuna patties and cook for 4 minutes. Turn the patties and cook for another 2 minutes. Season the patties lightly with salt and pepper to taste. Top the patties with the cheese slices, cover the skillet, and cook just until the cheese melts, 2 to 3 minutes. The tuna patties should remain slightly pink in the center.

Set the bottoms of the buns on plates. Place the patties on the buns and top each with a dollop of the remaining mayonnaise, 2 tomato slices, and 1 lettuce leaf. Set the bun tops in place and serve immediately.

Variation: The tuna burgers can be grilled over a charcoal fire or a gas grill and basted with purchased teriyaki glaze as they cook.

Ham and Crab Meat Salad Sandwiches

makes 8 big sandwiches

Crab and ham is an honorable southern pairing, and one that makes good eating sense. The sweet shellfish and the salty, smoky meat enhance each other wonderfully. I like to use unseeded pumpernickel or black bread for these, for a dramatic color contrast, but any sturdy, tender-crusted bread will work equally well. Handle the crab carefully, picking out as much cartilage as possible without breaking up the succulent lumps of meat.

¾ cup mayonnaise, fresh (page 89) or purchased
2 tablespoons fresh lemon juice
½ teaspoon salt
½ teaspoon hot pepper sauce
⅓ cup finely diced red sweet pepper
⅓ cup finely diced celery
⅓ cup thinly sliced green onions
1 pound jumbo lump crab meat, picked over for shell fragments
16 slices unseeded pumpernickel or black bread
1 pound smoked Black Forest ham, thinly sliced

In a medium bowl, whisk together the mayonnaise, lemon juice, salt, and hot pepper sauce. Stir in the red pepper, celery, and green onions. Gently fold in the crab meat. The crab meat salad can be prepared up to several hours in advance. Cover and refrigerate; return it to room temperature before proceeding.

Up to 30 minutes before serving, lay 8 slices of the bread on a work surface. Divide the crab meat mixture evenly among the bread slices, spreading it to the edges of the bread and using it all. Ruffle the sliced ham over the crab meat, dividing it evenly and using it all. Set the remaining slices of bread in place atop the ham. With a serrated knife, cut the sandwiches in half on the diagonal. Cover the sandwiches with plastic wrap and drape them with a damp paper towel until serving.

Oyster Po' Boy

makes 1 big sandwich, serving 2

The New Orleans po' boy--an overstuffed sandwich constructed on tender-crusted French bread--can be filled with any number of savory things (roast beef and brown gravy, to name one popular possibility), but few are more satisfying than the ones made with crisp, hot, deep-fried oysters. The oyster loaf is also sometimes called la mediatrice, or "the peacemaker," due to its reputation as the perfect gift from a tardy, possibly tipsy, husband to his irate spouse. The aphrodisiacal reputation of oysters may also have something to do with calming the marital waters, which is why this recipe serves only two.

4   cups corn oil
½   cup coarse-grind yellow cornmeal
1   teaspoon freshly ground black pepper
12   large shucked oysters
1   loaf soft Italian or French bread,
      14 to 16 inches long, ends trimmed,
      split horizontally
1   recipe Creole Dressing (page 91)
1   cup finely shredded crisp lettuce,
      such as romaine
4   thin slices ripe tomato

In a deep-fat fryer, or in a medium, heavy-bottomed saucepan fitted with a deep-fat thermometer, heat the corn oil to 375 degrees F. (The fryer or saucepan should be no more than half full.)

On a plate, stir together the cornmeal and pepper. Drain the oysters briefly to eliminate excess moisture, then dredge them in the cornmeal mixture until well coated.

With a slotted spoon, carefully lower the oysters into the hot fat. Cook, stirring the oysters once or twice, until they are crisp and golden, about 30 seconds. With a slotted spoon, transfer the oysters to paper towels and drain briefly.

Spread the cut sides of the bread loaf with the dressing, dividing it evenly and using it all. Arrange the hot oysters over the dressing on the bottom of the loaf. Top the oysters with the lettuce and then the tomatoes. Set the top of the loaf in place and, with the palm of your hand, gently flatten the sandwich. With a sharp knife, cut it in half on the diagonal and serve immediately.

Variation: For a combination loaf, replace half the oysters with 6 or 8 medium shrimp, peeled and deveined. Coat the shrimp with cornmeal and deep-fry as directed above for the oysters.

Lemony Lobster Club Sandwiches

makes 4 big sandwiches

Among the several specialties for which Anne Rosenzweig's Manhattan restaurant, Arcadia, is known, few get more press than her lobster club sandwich. Crisp, smoky bacon and lushly mayonnaised chunks of lobster are piled high on tender brioche toast, resulting in a triple-decker, knife-and-fork sandwich that daunts Arcadia's thin and stylish regulars not at all. My rendition is not so lofty (I like to pick up my clubs), but remains otherwise pure and true to its inspiration.

2   cups diced, cooked lobster meat
     (about 10 ounces), picked over (see note)
¾   cup Lemony Mayonnaise (page 89)
½   teaspoon salt
¼   teaspoon freshly ground black pepper
6   strips thick-cut bacon (about ½ pound total)
8   thick slices (each about 4 inches square)
     soft egg bread, such as brioche or challah
1   large, ripe tomato, cut into 8 thin slices
4   leaves crisp lettuce, such as romaine

In a medium bowl, combine the lobster meat, mayonnaise, salt, and pepper. Cover and hold at room temperature.

Preheat a broiler. Lay the bacon strips in a large skillet. Set the skillet over medium heat and cook, turning the bacon once or twice, until the strips are crisp, about 8 minutes. Drain on paper towels; cut the strips in half crosswise.

Meanwhile, under the broiler, toast the bread slices lightly on one side only.

Lay 4 slices of bread, toasted side down, on the work surface. Spread the lobster mixture evenly to the edges of the untoasted sides of each slice, using it all. Divide the half strips of bacon evenly over the lobster, then top the bacon with the tomato slices and lettuce leaves. Set the remaining bread slices, toasted side up, atop the lettuce. Flatten the sandwiches slightly with the palm of your hand. With a sharp knife, cut them in half on the diagonal. Serve immediately.

Note: Buy cooked lobster meat, use leftovers, or cook a lobster to order. To yield 10 ounces meat, bring about 3 inches of water to a boil in a large pot. Add a 1½-pound live lobster, cover, and cook until the shell is bright red, the tail is tightly curled and the flesh is just cooked through and opaque without being dry, about 12 minutes. Remove the lobster from the water and let cool to room temperature. Remove the meat from the shell. Slice or dice the larger pieces of meat.

Fresh Tuna Salad Sandwiches with Rosemary

makes 4 big sandwiches

Despite the convenience of canned tuna and the reassuring simplicity of
sandwiches made from it (see next page), I get a regular craving
for the freshly made sort outlined here. The tuna salad will be at its moist best
if the fish, once poached, is never refrigerated. Serve these
sandwiches with a salad of ripe summer tomatoes and a glass
of crisp white wine.

5	cups water
2	large fresh rosemary sprigs, plus 2½ teaspoons minced fresh rosemary
1	small lemon, thinly sliced
2	garlic cloves, thinly sliced
2	bay leaves
1½	teaspoons salt
1	teaspoon whole black peppercorns
1	pound tuna fillet or steak, in one piece, about 1½ inches thick
¾	cup mayonnaise, fresh (page 89) or purchased
¼	cup finely diced red onion
2	tablespoons fresh lemon juice
1	teaspoon minced lemon zest (yellow peel)
½	teaspoon freshly ground black pepper
2	loaves crusty Italian bread, each 14 to 16 inches long, ends trimmed, cut into four 6-inch-long sections and split horizontally
1	large, ripe tomato, cut into 8 thin slices
4	leaves crisp lettuce, such as romaine

In a medium, nonreactive pan, combine the water, rosemary sprigs, lemon slices, garlic cloves, bay leaves, 1 teaspoon of the salt, and the peppercorns. Set over medium heat, bring to a simmer, cover partially, and cook for 10 minutes. Add the tuna and simmer, turning the fish once, for 10 minutes. Remove the pan from the heat and let the tuna cool to room temperature in the poaching liquid.

Remove the tuna from the poaching liquid and pat it dry with paper towels. Remove and discard the skin (and the bones, if using steak); dice or flake the meat. In a medium bowl, mash together the minced rosemary and the remaining ½ teaspoon salt to form a rough paste. Whisk in the mayonnaise, then stir in the onion, lemon juice, lemon zest, and ground pepper. Fold in the diced tuna and adjust the seasoning.

Divide the tuna salad among the bottoms of the 4 sections of bread, spreading it evenly to the edges and using it all. Top the tuna salad with the tomato slices and the lettuce leaves. Set the tops of the bread sections in place. With a serrated knife, cut each sandwich in half crosswise on the diagonal. Serve immediately.

Twelve Terrific Tuna Salad Sandwiches

There is no nicer rut into which to get than that of the never-varying tuna sandwich. The satisfying ritual of can opener, fork, small bowl, and spoon (augmented by knife for those who use onion) is as reassuring as a Johnny Carson monologue, as calming as cookies and milk. Never measured (the physicality permanently imprinted by repetition onto neurons, muscles, and other internal pathways), one's tuna goes restfully together with an almost meditative blankness of mind, absence of thought or plan. And yet, consider: Whether scooped onto soda crackers (and thus not actually qualifying for this book) or incorporated into a big sandwich, tuna-melted, perhaps, even ruts were once new. While simplicity is an important part of the ritual, this is food we're talking about, and when same old same old no longer makes you as hungry as it once did, consider adopting, at least for a sandwich vacation or two, one of the following.

Purist

Mix together 1 can (6⅛ ounces) oil- or water-packed chunk light tuna, drained; 3 tablespoons mayonnaise, fresh (page 89) or purchased; 2 tablespoons minced yellow onion; 1 teaspoon fresh lemon juice; ½ teaspoon freshly ground black pepper; and ¼ teaspoon salt. Serve on toasted white bread, topped with sliced tomato and leaves of crisp lettuce. Makes 1 big sandwich.

Curried

Mix together 1 can (6⅛ ounces) oil- or water-packed chunk light tuna, drained; 3 tablespoons mayonnaise, fresh (page 89) or purchased; 2 tablespoons sliced green onions; 1 teaspoon Dijon mustard; 1½ teaspoons curry powder; ½ teaspoon freshly ground black pepper; and ¼ teaspoon salt. Serve on raisin bread, topped with mango chutney to taste. Makes 1 big sandwich.

Caper, Egg, and Anchovy

Mix together 1 can (6⅛ ounces) oil- or water-packed chunk light tuna, drained; 2 hard-cooked eggs, peeled and coarsely chopped; ⅓ cup mayonnaise, fresh (page 89) or purchased; 1 tablespoon well-drained small (nonpareil) capers; 2 teaspoons fresh lemon juice; 2 oil-packed anchovy fillets, minced; ½ teaspoon freshly ground black pepper; and ¼ teaspoon salt. Serve on focaccia, topped with sliced tomato and leaves of arugula. Makes 2 big sandwiches.

Nacho

Mix together 1 can (6⅛ ounces) oil- or water-packed chunk light tuna, drained; ½ cup (2 ounces) coarsely grated sharp Cheddar cheese; ⅓ cup mayonnaise, fresh (page 89) or purchased; ¼ cup minced, drained pickled jalapeños; 3 tablespoons sliced green onions;

2 teaspoons fresh lime juice; and ¼ teaspoon salt. Serve on crusty white bread, topped with sliced tomatoes and leaves of lettuce. Makes 2 big sandwiches.

Caraway

Mix together 1 can (6⅛ ounces) oil- or water-packed chunk light tuna, drained; 3 tablespoons mayonnaise, fresh (page 89) or purchased; 2 tablespoons minced red onion; 1 tablespoon honey mustard; 1 teaspoon caraway seeds; 1 teaspoon fresh lemon juice; ½ teaspoon freshly ground black pepper; and ¼ teaspoon salt. Serve on toasted seedless rye bread. Makes 1 big sandwich.

Sweet Mustardy Dill

Mix together 1 can (6⅛ ounces) oil- or water-packed chunk light tuna, drained; 2 tablespoons mayonnaise, fresh (page 89) or purchased; 2 tablespoons honey mustard; 1 tablespoon minced fresh dill; 1 teaspoon fresh lemon juice; ½ teaspoon freshly ground black pepper; and ¼ teaspoon salt. Serve on marbled pumpernickel-rye bread. Makes 1 big sandwich.

Lemon-Garden

Mix together 1 can (6⅛ ounces) oil- or water-packed chunk light tuna, drained; ½ cup coarsely chopped, crisp-cooked broccoli; ⅓ cup mayonnaise, fresh (page 89) or purchased; ⅓ cup diced raw carrot; 2 table-spoons chopped red or green onion; 1 teaspoon fresh lemon juice; 1 teaspoon minced lemon zest (yellow peel); ½ teaspoon freshly ground black pepper; and ¼ teaspoon salt. Serve on moist, heavy multigrain bread and top with sliced tomatoes. Makes 1 big sandwich.

Joan's Uptown

Mix together 1 can (6⅛ ounces) oil- or water-packed chunk light tuna, drained; 1 hard-cooked egg, peeled and coarsely chopped; ¼ cup mayonnaise, fresh (page 89) or purchased; 10 pitted California ripe black olives, sliced; 2 tablespoons sweet pickle relish, drained; 1 tablespoon minced fresh chives; 1 teaspoon Dijon mustard; ½ teaspoon freshly ground black pepper; ¼ teaspoon salt; and a pinch of celery seeds. Serve on San Francisco sourdough toast. Makes 2 big sandwiches.

Pesto

Mix together 1 can (6⅛ ounces) oil- or water-packed chunk light tuna, drained; 3 tablespoons pesto; 1 tablespoon mayonnaise, fresh (page 89) or purchased; 2 teaspoons fresh lemon juice; ½ teaspoon freshly ground black pepper; and a pinch of salt. Serve on toasted semolina bread and top with sliced tomatoes and romaine lettuce. Makes 1 big sandwich.

The Ekuses' Oniony-Ginger

Mix together 1 can (6⅛ ounces) oil- or water-packed chunk light tuna, drained; ¼ cup minced yellow or red onion; 2 tablespoons plus 2 teaspoons mayonnaise, fresh (page 89) or purchased; 2 tablespoons plus 2 teaspoons liquid from Asian pickled ginger; ½ teaspoon freshly ground black pepper; ½ teaspoon dry mustard; and ¼ teaspoon salt. Serve on toasted challah bread. Makes 1 big sandwich.

Radish-Ranch

Mix together 1 can (6⅛ ounces) oil- or water-packed chunk light tuna, drained; 4 crisp radishes, trimmed and diced; 3 tablespoons bottled ranch dressing; 3 tablespoons sliced green onions; ½ teaspoon freshly ground black pepper; and a pinch of salt. Serve on seeded whole-grain bread. Makes 1 big sandwich.

Toasted Sesame

Mix together 1 can (6⅛ ounces) oil- or water-packed chunk light tuna, drained; ¼ cup sliced green onions; 3 tablespoons mayonnaise, fresh (page 89) or purchased; 1 tablespoon toasted sesame seeds; 1 teaspoon Asian sesame oil; 1 teaspoon fresh lemon juice; ½ teaspoon freshly ground black pepper; and ¼ teaspoon salt. Serve on a crusty hard roll, topped with radish sprouts or bean sprouts. Makes 1 big sandwich.

Artichoke-Garlic

Mix together 1 can (6⅛ ounces) oil- or water-packed chunk light tuna, drained; 1 jar (6½ ounces) marinated artichoke hearts, drained and chopped; 2 tablespoons minced yellow or red onion; 2 tablespoons mayonnaise, fresh (page 89) or purchased; 1 tablespoon olive oil; 1 small garlic clove, crushed through a press; 1 teaspoon red wine vinegar; ½ teaspoon freshly ground black pepper; and ¼ teaspoon salt. Serve on sections of a baguette, topped with slices of tomato and sprigs of watercress. Makes 2 big sandwiches.

Crisp Salmon Fillet Sandwiches
with Green Chile Mayonnaise

makes 4 big sandwiches

Other rich fish (catfish, for example) can be substituted, but the ready availability of farmed salmon, its modest price, and built-in celebratory appeal make it the ideal choice for these festive sandwiches. For the best flavor, choose unspiced corn chips made from real tortillas, not extruded snack chips, even if this means you must fry up your own.

2   eggs
2   tablespoons milk
1   cup finely crushed corn tortilla chips
⅓   cup unbleached all-purpose flour
⅔   cup corn oil
4   skinless salmon fillets, 6 ounces each
     (see note), at room temperature
     Salt
     Freshly ground black pepper
4   Nice Buns (page 87) or any large,
     good-quality crusty sandwich roll,
     split horizontally
1   medium-sized ripe tomato, trimmed
     and thinly sliced
1   recipe Green Chile Mayonnaise (page 90)

In a shallow bowl, whisk together the eggs and milk. Measure the flour onto a medium plate. Measure the crushed corn chips into a wide, shallow dish, like a pie plate.

In a large skillet over medium heat, warm the corn oil. Meanwhile, season the salmon fillets on both sides with salt and pepper to taste. One at a time, dip the fillets into the flour, shaking off the excess, then into the egg mixture, and finally into the crushed corn chips, coating them heavily and evenly. Carefully slip the coated fillets into the hot oil and cook, rearranging them once or twice to promote even cooking, until crisp and lightly browned on one side, about 4 minutes. With a spatula, turn the fillets and cook until crisp and browned on the second side, another 3 to 4 minutes; the salmon inside the crust should be moist and just beginning to flake.

Set the bottoms of the buns on plates. With a slotted spatula, transfer the fillets to paper towels to drain briefly, then place them on the bottoms. Top each fillet with some of the chile mayonnaise, dividing it evenly and using it all. Top the fillets with the tomato slices, set the bun tops in place, and serve immediately.

Note: To promote even cooking, ask that the fillets be cut from the thick end of 4 separate smallish whole fillets, yielding more or less identical pieces of fish about ¾ inch at their thickest point.

Smoked Salmon, Cucumber, and Cream Cheese Sandwiches

makes 4 big sandwiches

Big sandwiches are rarely elegant sandwiches, although these come close. Don't be tempted to make them dainty--this isn't a tea party--but do use the best (imported) smoked salmon available. A moist, dense whole-wheat bread makes a fine textural contrast with the silky fish, but white or black bread would also be a good choice. The sliced onion, which transforms the sandwich from something refined into something vivid and earthy, is optional.

1	hothouse (English) cucumber, trimmed and thinly sliced
2	tablespoons red wine vinegar
5	teaspoons sugar
1	teaspoon salt
½	pound cream cheese, preferably stabilizer free, at room temperature
8	slices whole-wheat bread
1	pound smoked salmon, thinly sliced, brought just to room temperature
	Freshly ground black pepper
1	small red onion, thinly sliced (optional)

In a medium, nonreactive bowl, combine the cucumber slices, vinegar, sugar, and salt. Cover and let stand at room temperature, stirring once or twice, for 1 hour.

Spread the cream cheese thickly and evenly over 4 slices of the bread, using it all. Ruffle the salmon slices over the cream cheese. With a slotted spoon, remove the cucumber slices from their marinade and arrange them evenly over the salmon, dividing them evenly and using them all. Season the cucumber slices to taste with pepper. If you are using the onion, separate the slices into rings and scatter them over the cucumber slices. Set the remaining 4 slices of bread in place atop the onions. With a long, sharp knife, cut the sandwiches in half on the diagonal. Serve immediately.

Soft-shell Crab Sandwiches with Tabasco Toasted-Pecan Mayonnaise

makes 2 big sandwiches

Few big sandwiches are as satisfying as these, in which buttery, crunchy, sea-juicy crabs are served between big slabs of toasted egg bread and lavished with a nutty, peppery mayonnaise. Of the handful of recipes in this book for which, despite what I say, only homemade mayo will really do, this one is foremost: Do yourself a favor and whisk up a batch of the real thing. You and your lucky guest will be glad you did.

⅓ cup unbleached all-purpose flour
½ teaspoon freshly ground black pepper
¼ teaspoon salt
½ stick (4 tablespoons) unsalted butter
4 medium-sized soft-shell crabs, dressed
4 large slices challah or brioche bread
1 recipe Tabasco Toasted-Pecan Mayonnaise (page 90)

In a wide, shallow plate, stir together the flour, pepper, and salt.

Preheat a broiler. In a large skillet over medium heat, melt the butter. Meanwhile, dredge the crabs in the seasoned flour, coating them evenly; shake off the excess. When the butter foams, lay the crabs in the skillet (they may spatter) and cook uncovered, turning once, until they are crisp and golden, about 3 minutes per side. With a spatula, transfer the crabs to a plate.

Meanwhile, under the broiler, toast the bread slices lightly on one side only. Lay 2 slices, untoasted side up, on a work surface. Lay 2 crabs, overlapping them slightly, on each bread slice. Top the crabs with the mayonnaise, dividing it evenly and using it all. Set the remaining 2 slices of bread, untoasted side down, atop the mayonnaise.

With the palm of a hand, flatten the sandwiches slightly. With a sharp knife, cut the sandwiches in half on the diagonal. Serve immediately.

Shrimp on a Shingle

makes 4 big sandwiches

This is a hard call--is it even a sandwich? Is creamed chipped beef on toast, the military-industrial inspiration for the title, a sandwich? Shouldn't sandwiches, technically speaking, be pick-up-able? But then, one should not, after all, pick up an open-faced hot turkey or roast beef sandwich, however messy fun that might, at first, seem to be. Or is a sandwich defined by the inclusion of bread? This elegant, creamy, slightly spicy shrimp-studded sauce could well be tossed with twelve ounces of, say, al dente penne, rather than spooned over crisp toast, except that then, I guess, it wouldn't be a sandwich. But where does that leave biscuits with sausage gravy? Creamed chicken on waffles? Sautéed wild mushrooms over crisp fried polenta? Oh hell, let's eat.

½   stick (4 tablespoons) unsalted butter
1   pound large shrimp (about 28), peeled and deveined
1   heavy red sweet pepper, stemmed, seeded, and diced
½   cup diced fennel bulb
4   garlic cloves, minced
½   teaspoon dried basil, crumbled
¼   teaspoon red pepper flakes
1   tablespoon unbleached all-purpose flour
1½   cups whipping cream
½   cup canned crushed tomatoes with added purée

¾   teaspoon salt
1   cup frozen petite peas, thawed and drained
¼   cup grated Parmesan cheese, preferably imported
3   tablespoons minced fennel fronds
4   large, thick slices crusty country-style white bread, lightly toasted and halved crosswise
2   ounces prosciutto, thinly sliced and cut crosswise into julienne strips

In a large skillet over medium heat, melt the butter. When it foams, add the shrimp and cook, tossing and stirring often, until pink and curled but not cooked through, about 2 minutes. With a slotted spoon, transfer the shrimp to a bowl.

Stir the diced red pepper, fennel, garlic, basil, and red pepper flakes into the butter remaining in the skillet. Cover and cook over medium heat, stirring once or twice, until lightly colored and almost tender, about 10 minutes. Stir in the flour and cook, stirring often, for 2 minutes. Stir in the cream, tomatoes, and salt and bring to a simmer. Add the shrimp, any juices from the bowl, and the peas to the skillet and cook, stirring once or twice, until the shrimp are heated through and just fully cooked, about 2 minutes. Remove from the heat, stir in the Parmesan and the fennel fronds, and adjust the seasoning.

Arrange the pieces of toast, overlapping them slightly, in 4 wide, shallow bowls. Spoon the shrimp and the sauce over the toast, dividing them evenly and using them all. Scatter the prosciutto evenly over the shrimp.

Serve immediately.

Garden Variety

Meatless Muffaletta

Scrambled Egg Heroes with Potatoes, Spinach, and Cheese

Some Classic Big Sandwiches Defined

Brazos Bruschettas

Griddled Tomato, Pesto, and Three-Cheese Sandwiches

Sandwiches Caprese

Lentil Salad Pitas with Tomatoes and Feta

Focaccia Sandwiches with Mushrooms, Garlicky Greens, and Goat Cheese

Pan Bagnat

Oven-Baked Eggplant Parmigiana Heroes

Russian Radish, Sour Cream, and Pumpernicke Sandwiches

Meatless Muffaletta

makes 1 large sandwich, serving 4

The muffaletta (say muffa-<u>lah</u>-tah) is a specialty of New Orleans and typically features a tangy olive salad, sliced Italian deli meats, and cheeses piled onto a large round loaf. The loaf is then quartered, producing sandwiches that are real fistfuls of zesty eating – a quality that is not diminished when the meats are omitted. Olive and pepper salads can be purchased at Italian-style delicatessens, but decent versions are also available in jars in the olive and pickle sections of many supermarkets. For best results, the bland soybean oil in which they are packed is here replaced with good olive oil. Hot peppers, balsamic vinegar, garlic, and fresh oregano add extra zip.

1   jar (9¾ ounces) olive salad, drained
1   jar (9½ ounces) mixed pepper salad, drained
½   cup sliced, drained pickled hot cherry peppers
3   tablespoons olive oil
2½   tablespoons balsamic vinegar
2   tablespoons minced fresh oregano
2   garlic cloves, crushed through a press
1   round semolina or sourdough loaf, about
     7 inches in diameter and 3 inches thick
1   pound smoked mozzarella cheese, thickly
     sliced, at room temperature

In a medium bowl, combine the olive salad, pepper salad, cherry peppers, olive oil, balsamic vinegar, oregano, and garlic. Let stand at room temperature, stirring once or twice, for 30 minutes.

With a serrated knife, cut the semolina loaf in half horizontally. With your fingers, remove some of the soft interior crumb from each half, leaving a shell about 1 inch thick. (Reserve the crumb for another use.)

Spoon about two-thirds of the olive mixture into the bottom half of the loaf. Arrange the sliced mozzarella in an overlapping layer atop the olive salad. Fill the hollow in the top half with the remaining olive mixture and invert it atop the cheese.

Wrap the sandwich in plastic, weight it (with a heavy pot lid, for example), and let it stand at room temperature for 1 hour. Remove the weight, and, with a serrated knife, cut the sandwich into quarters. Serve immediately.

Variation: To make a traditional muffaletta, replace the smoked mozzarella with about ¾ pound thinly sliced assorted meats (mortadella, *sopressata*, salami) and ¼ pound thinly sliced processed provolone.

51

Scrambled Egg Heroes with Potatoes, Spinach, and Cheese

makes 4 big sandwiches

Those who dip their toast into their breakfast eggs will readily appreciate the appeal of a sandwich of crusty bread filled with warm scrambled eggs. Few combinations are so squishy and comforting, whether served for breakfast, lunch, or supper. (Contrariwise, the egg filling can also be cooled to room temperature before the sandwiches are assembled; wrapped individually in waxed paper; and served, upon arrival, with applications of plenty of hot salsa, they make admirable picnic fare.)

2   large boiling potatoes (about 1 pound total), peeled and cut into ½-inch dice

3¼   teaspoons salt

2   tablespoons unsalted butter

1   tablespoon corn oil

10   large eggs

¾   teaspoon freshly ground black pepper

2   cups finely chopped fresh spinach

1   cup grated mild, white, melting cheese such as Havarti

2   loaves crusty Italian bread, each 14 to 16 inches long, ends trimmed, cut into four 6-inch-long sections, and split horizontally

In a medium saucepan, cover the potatoes with cold water. Stir in 2 teaspoons of the salt, set over medium heat, and bring to a simmer. Cook uncovered, stirring once or twice, until the potatoes are just tender, about 6 minutes. Drain thoroughly. The potatoes can be prepared up to 1 day ahead. Cover and refrigerate them; return them to room temperature before proceeding.

In a large, heavy skillet over medium heat, melt together the butter and corn oil. Add the potatoes and cook uncovered, stirring occasionally, until they are crisp and golden, 10 to 12 minutes.

Meanwhile, in a large bowl, briefly whisk the eggs. Whisk in the remaining 1¼ teaspoons salt and the pepper.

When the potatoes are crisp, pour the eggs over them. Cook, stirring often, until the eggs are partially set, about 3 minutes. Add the spinach and cook, stirring often, for 1 minute. Stir in the cheese, remove the skillet from the heat, cover, and let stand for 1 minute.

Spoon the hot egg mixture into the bread sections, dividing it evenly and using it all. Serve immediately.

Some Classic Big Sandwiches Defined

Depending on where you live, and the big sandwiches to which you have grown attached, this list will either be full of old friends, intriguing new possibilities, or both. The loosey-goosey nature of sandwich making means generalizations are risky--your hoagie may be my sub--but the following are as accurate as it is possible to be without taking all the fun out of sandwich making and eating.

Barbecue

Always served on cheap sliced white bread, barbecue sandwiches display regional variations in the meat that is smoked and the sauce that is applied thereto. In the Southeast, barbecue is pork shoulder, chopped or shredded ("pulled"); the sauce varies from mustardy tart to sweetly hot. In Kentucky, the meat is mutton, the sauce usually red and fiery. In Texas, pork shoulder may be offered (also spareribs and spicy sausages known as hot links), but the star is beef brisket. Texans (like barbecue purists elsewhere) are known to skip the sauce altogether, but they are usually offered thin, red, tart medium-hot stuff in commercial establishments, thicker, sweeter, hotter, chile powder--seasoned stuff in homes or catered 'que events.

Origin: Throughout the South and much of the Southwest.

Beef-on-Weck

Thinly sliced roast beef on a salt-crusted caraway hard roll (Kümmelweck). The cut sides of the roll are optionally dipped into the beef juices.

See also: Loosemeats, French Dip.

Origin: Upstate New York.

BLT

Bacon, lettuce, and tomato on toasted white bread, with mayonnaise. "Lettuce is sometimes added," wrote James Beard, "but why?" Possibly because BT sounds funny. Optional: Melt American cheese atop the bacon before completing the sandwich. See also: Club, BLT & G(uacamole) (page 24).

Origin: National.

Club

Sliced roast, poached, or grilled chicken with tomato, lettuce, and crisp bacon on toasted white bread, with mayonnaise. First mentioned in print circa 1903; variously ascribed to the kitchens of men's social clubs, two-decker club cars on streamliner trains, or the Saratoga Club, Saratoga, New York, where Saratoga chips (fresh potato chips) and the card game Canfield Solitaire were invented. The double-decker (three slices of toast, two layers of filling) is now the norm, but James Beard thought it a "bastardized horror." Had there been, for some apocalyptic reason, no hamburger, the club would surely have become the all-American sandwich. See also: Monte Cristo; Lemony Lobster Club Sandwiches (page 38). Variations: Sliced roast beef, boiled ham, turkey breast, and American or Swiss cheese popularly—if dubiously —join or replace the chicken. Grilled fish clubs have been enjoyed. Flavored mayonnaises (aioli, herbal, sun-dried tomato) add contemporary interest.

Origin: National.

Coney Island

You can get a hot dog on Coney Island, but it comes from Nathan's and it's called a frank (or, almost as likely, an Italian sausage sandwich). For a Coney Island qua Coney Island (a garnished hot dog, especially a chili dog), you must head west into Chicago, Cincinnati, and other Greek-settled communities, where nostalgic and sensibly mercenary immigrants from the East Coast made the Coney into an institution. It must be regretfully noted that in Cincinnati's otherwise estimable chili parlors, what passes for a frankfurter appears to be a Vienna sausage, straight from the can.

Origin: Midwest, via Brooklyn.

Croque-Madame and Croque-Monsieur

Madame consists of sliced chicken and Gruyère cheese on egg-battered or merely well-buttered firm white French sandwich bread (pain de mie); monsieur replaces the chicken with ham. Either may be lightly spread with good Dijon mustard before being closed up. The sandwiches are griddled, either in a skillet or clamped into a hinged, stove-top mold, occasionally available from fancy kitchenware catalogs, designed to impress the sandwiches with an elegant scallop design. See also: Monte Cristo.

Origin: France.

Cuban

A Miami, Florida, specialty. A long loaf of soft Italian or Cuban bread is split. It may be lightly spread with mayonnaise, mustard, or both. Thinly sliced Swiss cheese, boiled ham, and roast pork (or roast beef) are layered onto the bottom. Sour pickle chips top all. The sandwich is closed, buttered on the *outside*, and squash-grilled between the heated surfaces of a sandwich toaster. Variation: Bacon, lettuce, and tomato join or replace some of the other ingredients, as desired. This Cuban is not grilled. See also: Hero, Hoagie, Grinder, Sub.

Origin: Miami, via Havana.

Denver (Western)

Lively predecessor to the Egg McMuffin. Denver omelet (eggs, ham or bacon, sautéed bell pepper, and onions) on a toasted, buttered roll. Variations: Add cheese. Add jalapeños. Omit the onions for an eastern sandwich.

Origin: Western United States.

Falafel

Deep-fried fritters of soaked, ground chick-peas (garbanzos), frequently seasoned with garlic and cumin, served in pita breads with lettuce, tomato, and a thin tahini (sesame) sauce.

Origin: Eastern Mediterranean, especially Egypt and Israel.

French Dip
Thinly sliced roast beef on a hard roll. At Phillipe The Original, in Los Angeles, home (in the West, at least) of this combination, the cut sides of the roll are dipped into unthickened natural gravy—"au jus"—before the sandwich is assembled. (See: Beef-on-Weck, Loosemeats.) Elsewhere, separate ramekins of oniony beef broth may be offered for dunking. In Los Angeles, Phillipe's own fiery yellow mustard is part of the success of the sandwich. Similarly: Beef Manhattan in Kansas, Italian Beef in Chicago.

Origin: National.

Gyro
Thinly sliced meat from a rotisserie-grilled cylinder of processed meats, usually a combination of lamb and beef. Served tucked into pita bread with lettuce, tomatoes, and a thin, garlicky tahini (sesame) sauce. Similarly: Skewered, grilled beef or lamb or thinly sliced grilled lamb is used in place of the gyro meat, to produce a souvlaki sandwich.

Origin: Greece.

Hero, Hoagie, Grinder, Sub
Also: Torpedo, Wedge, Bomber, Zep. Various cold or hot regional combinations of cold cuts, roast meats, cheeses, meatballs, sausages, veal parmigiana, sweet and/or hot peppers, lettuce, tomato, oil-and-vinegar dressings, mayonnaise, mustard, tomato sauce ("gravy"), brown gravy, etc., layered onto long Italian loaves. Further generalization is risky, but hoagies are generally cold sandwiches, while subs and heroes are hot.

See also: Philly Cheesesteak, Cuban, Oyster Po' Boy (page 37), Meatless Muffaletta (page 51), Scrambled Egg Heroes with Potatoes, Spinach, and Cheese (page 52), Oven-Baked Eggplant Parmigiana Heroes (page 64).

Origin: Italian-American northeastern United States.

Iowa Fried Tenderloins
Huge, thinly pounded pork tenderloins, breaded in crushed cracker crumbs ("chicken fried") or cornmeal, then fried crisp. Served on, but badly overhanging, a soft bun, with lettuce, tomato, and mayonnaise or Russian dressing, plus optional mustard. At The White Mill, in Monmouth, Illinois, according to Jane and Michael Stern, one may order "sandy mash"—a halved tenderloin sandwich, served on either side of a steaming mound of mashed potatoes and gravy.

Origin: Midwest, especially Iowa.

Keftedes
Grilled or sautéed lamb (or beef mixed with pork) meatballs, well seasoned, sometimes with cinnamon, on crusty rolls or tucked into pita, with lettuce, tomatoes, parsley or mint, and yogurt.

Origin: Greece.

Lobster (or Crab) Rolls

Quintessential shore cuisine. Many sweet chunks of lobster or crab, served hot (drenched with melted butter, and preferred by connoisseurs) or cold (dressed with mayonnaise, crunched up with celery) on plain old hot dog rolls (buttered and toasted, if desired), which rapidly dissolve under the onslaught of well-lubricated shellfish. Potato chips and pickles may accompany; amenities are few (most lobster rolls are eaten outdoors, at picnic tables, with only paper napkins for mopping up).

Origin: New England, especially Connecticut.

Loosemeats

Also: Maid-Rites, taverns, Charlie Boys, Tastees. "Little burger pebbles on a bun—like a sloppy joe without the slop," according to the Sterns. Skillet-browned (well, grayed) ground beef, plus onions, brown sugar, tomato juice, Worcestershire sauce, etc., served on sliced white bread, which may first be dragged through the grease that rises to the top of the meat.
See also: Beef-on-Weck, French Dip, Proustian Sloppy Joes (page 27). Cheez Whiz can be extruded atop the meats before the sandwich is closed, at least on "Roseanne," which has done as much for these sandwiches as "Cheers" did for beer.

Origin: Ye Olde Tavern Inn, Sioux City, Iowa, (circa 1934), by way of Hollywood and of Lanford, Illinois.

Louisville Hot Brown

Created by Fred K. Schmidt, a chef at Louisville, Kentucky's elegant Brown Hotel, in the 1930s. Consisting of sliced turkey over toast points, topped with hollandaise and mornay sauces, broiled until bubbly, then garnished with sliced tomato and crisp bacon, it is still served at the Brown, and elsewhere in town.
Variations: Be damned!

Origin: Louisville, Kentucky.

Monte Cristo

Double-decker sandwich of ham and cheese, and sometimes chicken also, dipped into a thin French toast-type batter and griddled, or into a thickened fritter-type batter and deep-fried. Served with various sweet garnishes, including currant jelly, powdered sugar, and/or maple syrup.
See also: Club, Mozzarella in Carrozza, Peppery French-Toasted Ham-and-Apple-Butter Sandwiches (page 78).

Origin: Unknown.

Mozzarella in Carrozza

Batter-dipped, sometimes skewered, deep-fried sandwiches of bread and mozzarella cheese, served with a hot caper-and-anchovy sauce.
See also: Monte Cristo, Spiedies.

Origin: Italy.

Navaho Fry Bread "Tacos"

Qualifying as sandwiches because they are based upon thick rounds of fried bread, versions of these tacos are also prepared by the Hopi, the Pima, the Tohono O'Odham, the Tigua, and other southwestern tribes.

Similar to sopaipillas, but usually yeast-raised, the fry bread rounds are topped with cooked pinto beans or fiery pork, beef, or lamb chile, along with lettuce, cheese, tomatoes, and other toppings. Attempt to pick up these tacos at your own peril.

Origin: Southwestern United States.

Philly Cheesesteak

Few big sandwiches are so highly regarded, or so squishy and fattening. Greasy griddled onions, fried (previously frozen) paper-thin sandwich steaks, plus optional Cheez Whiz, sautéed red and green sweet peppers, and hot sauce, on an Italian hoagie roll. Prime purveyors: Pat's (also claimant to invention of the cheesesteak, circa 1930), Mike and Carol's.

Origin: South Philadelphia.

Spiedies

Long-marinated chunks of lamb, beef, pork, or chicken, which are skewered, grilled, then slid off onto soft white or Italian bread, are a specialty of Binghamton, New York, and environs, where immigrant (read Italian) workers manned the shoe factories. According to Susan Wyler, the name comes from *spiedini*, Italian for "skewers."

Origin: Italian-American east-central New York State and northwestern Pennsylvania.

St. Louis Fried Brain Sandwiches

Beer-battered, deep-fried, and served on rye bread with pickles, onions, and mustard. Purists eschew chopped or ground brains, proudly serving each diner an intact half brain. Drink beer.

Origin: St. Louis, Missouri.

Wisconsin Bratwurst

Meaty fresh pork sausages (bearing no resemblance to the white sausages also sold under that name elsewhere in this country as well as in Germany; those sausages are known as weisswurst in Wisconsin—are you following all this?), charcoal grilled and traditionally served on a hard, crusty kaiserlike roll known as a *Semmel*. Wisconsin brats are often kept warm in a pan of buttered beer. Mustard, sauerkraut, and other sausage-friendly accompaniments are recommended.

Origin: Wisconsin, especially Sheboygan.

Brazos Bruschettas

makes 4 big sandwiches

While for much of the year tomatoes play an essential but supporting role in many of my big sandwiches, when summer reaches its blowsy peak, and gardens and markets are flooded with crimson, vine-ripened perfection, they become the stars. This slightly Texas twist on an open-faced Italian favorite makes a fine light lunch or supper (or the sandwiches can be served as a first course, preceding something hot and smoky from the grill).

2 large, ripe tomatoes (about 1 pound total)
⅓ cup olive oil
1 tablespoon balsamic vinegar
1 tablespoon red wine vinegar
2 garlic cloves, peeled and mashed
¾ teaspoon salt
1 large ripe Haas avocado, pitted, peeled, and cut into ½-inch dice
⅓ pound smoked mozzarella cheese, cut into ½-inch dice, at room temperature
½ cup julienned fresh basil leaves, plus 4 fresh basil sprigs, for garnish
¾ teaspoon freshly ground black pepper
4 large, thick slices crusty country-style bread, lightly toasted

With a serrated knife, cut the tomatoes into ½-inch chunks. In a medium bowl, combine the tomato chunks and any juices with the olive oil, balsamic vinegar, red wine vinegar, garlic, and salt. Cover and let stand at room temperature for 30 minutes.

Stir the avocado, mozzarella, julienned basil, and pepper into the tomato mixture. Set a slice of warm toasted bread on each of 4 plates. Spoon the tomato mixture, including the juices, over the toasted bread, dividing it evenly and using it all. Garnish each sandwich with a sprig of basil and serve immediately.

Variation: Brush the bread with additional olive oil and toast it on the grill.

Griddled Tomato, Pesto, and Three-Cheese Sandwiches

makes 4 big sandwiches

The ideal pairing of tomatoes and cheese can also be enjoyed in a hot sandwich, as illustrated here. The brief ingredient list requires the best possible ingredients (especially ripe juicy tomatoes and a crusty, flavorful bread), but good-quality purchased pesto can certainly be used in place of homemade. Serve the hot, crunchy, cheese-pully sandwiches with a crisp, cool green salad.

¾ cup ricotta cheese

¼ cup pesto sauce

2 tablespoons grated imported Parmesan cheese

½ teaspoon red pepper flakes

¼ teaspoon salt

8 large slices crusty country-style bread

10 ounces smoked processed provolone, cut into 8 thin slices

1 medium-sized, ripe tomato, cut into 4 thin slices

⅓ cup olive oil

Put the ricotta in a fine-mesh strainer over a bowl and let drain for 30 minutes; discard the liquid.

In a small bowl, stir together the ricotta, pesto, Parmesan, red pepper and salt. Lay 4 slices of bread on a work surface. Top each with 1 slice provolone. Lay a tomato slice over the provolone on each sandwich. Top the tomato with the ricotta mixture, dividing it evenly and using it all. Top the ricotta with the remaining provolone slices. Set the remaining 4 bread slices atop the provolone and press gently with the palm of your hand to bring the ricotta mixture just to the edges of the sandwiches.

Set a large skillet (or griddle) over medium heat. Brush about half the olive oil over the tops of the sandwiches, dividing it evenly. Set the sandwiches, oiled side down, in the skillet, cover, and cook until the bottoms are crisp and browned, about 5 minutes. Brush the tops of the sandwiches with the remaining olive oil, dividing it evenly, turn them, cover the skillet, and cook until the provolone has melted, the bottoms are crisp and browned, and the sandwiches are heated through, another 3 to 4 minutes.

Transfer to a cutting board. With a serrated knife, cut the sandwiches in half on the diagonal. Serve immediately.

Sandwiches Caprese

makes 4 big sandwiches

These sandwiches are based on the classic <u>insalata caprese</u>, whose slices of milky, fresh mozzarella and juicy, ripe tomatoes, garnished with fresh basil, replicate the colors of the Italian flag. The vibrant trio is summer itself, needing little else save a glossing of oil and a dribble of vinegar (which you may wish to omit, if your tomatoes are sweet-tart perfection), all piled into a crusty loaf.

2   loaves crusty Italian bread, each about 14 inches long, ends trimmed, cut into four 6-inch-long sections, and partially split horizontally
1   pound fresh mozzarella cheese, thickly sliced, at room temperature
24   large fresh basil leaves
4   large, ripe tomatoes (about 2 pounds total), thickly sliced
4   teaspoons olive oil
4   teaspoons balsamic vinegar
½   teaspoon salt
½   teaspoon freshly ground black pepper

Lay the sections of bread on a work surface. Arrange the mozzarella slices, overlapping them slightly, on the bottom of each section. Arrange the basil leaves in a single layer over the mozzarella. Arrange the tomato slices, overlapping them slightly, over the basil. Drizzle the tomato slices evenly with the olive oil and vinegar. Sprinkle the tomatoes evenly with the salt and pepper.

Close the sandwiches and press gently with the palm of your hand to flatten them slightly. With a serrated knife, cut the sandwiches in half on the diagonal. Serve immediately.

Lentil Salad Pitas with Tomatoes and Feta

makes 8 big sandwiches

Many foods are described as "meaty" or as being as satisfying as meat, and while lentils don't often appear on that list, I think they should. These spicy and completely satisfying lentil-stuffed pitas are one good illustration of my point, and never fail to please even ardent carnivores.

1½   cups brown lentils, picked over and rinsed
2½   teaspoons salt
2   cups packed fresh basil leaves
3   tablespoons balsamic vinegar
3   tablespoons fresh lemon juice
1   fresh jalapeño chile, stemmed and chopped
3   garlic cloves, chopped
2   tablespoons Dijon mustard
½   teaspoon freshly ground black pepper
½   cup olive oil
¼   pound feta cheese, preferably imported and made from sheep's milk, drained and crumbled
½   cup diced red onions
2   large, ripe tomatoes, each cut into 4 thick slices, and the slices halved crosswise
8   pita breads, each 6 inches in diameter, halved crosswise
½   bunch watercress

Fill a medium saucepan three-quarters full of water, set it over high heat, and bring to a boil. Stir in the lentils and 2 teaspoons of the salt, reduce the heat to medium, cover partially, and simmer, stirring once or twice, until the lentils are just tender, about 25 minutes.

Meanwhile, in a food processor, combine the basil, vinegar, lemon juice, jalapeño, garlic, mustard, pepper, and the remaining ½ teaspoon salt. Process until smooth. With the motor running, gradually add the olive oil through the feed tube; the dressing will thicken.

Drain the lentils and transfer them to a medium bowl. Immediately pour the dressing over the hot lentils. Cool to room temperature, stirring occasionally. The lentil salad can be prepared 1 day ahead. Cover and refrigerate; return it to room temperature before proceeding.

Preheat the oven to 400 degrees F. Stir the feta and red onions into the lentil salad. Lay the pitas directly on the oven rack and bake until hot and flexible, 2 to 3 minutes. Place 2 pita halves on each of 8 plates. Tuck a halved tomato slice and a sprig or two of watercress into each pita half. Spoon about ¼ cup lentil salad into each pita half. Serve immediately.

Variation: Crumbled fresh goat cheese can be used in place of the feta. Chopped, pitted Greek black olives can be used along with, or in place of, the feta.

Focaccia Sandwiches with Mushrooms, Garlicky Greens, and Goat Cheese

makes 1 big sandwich, serving 4

This sturdy sandwich combines meaty portobello mushrooms, garlicky and slightly bitter broccoli rabe, and tangy goat cheese. For best results, look for a thick, round <u>focaccia</u> bread that can be split horizontally.

7	tablespoons olive oil
5 or 6	large portobello mushroom caps (about ¾ pound total)
	Salt
3	garlic cloves, minced
¼	teaspoon red pepper flakes
1¼	pounds broccoli rabe, tough stems removed, rinsed but not dried
1	round *focaccia*, about 9 inches in diameter and 2 inches thick, split horizontally
6	ounces mild fresh goat cheese, at room temperature
	Freshly ground black pepper

Position a rack in the middle of an oven and preheat to 400 degrees F. In a large skillet over medium heat, warm 2 tablespoons of the olive oil. Add 2 or 3 of the mushroom caps, season with a pinch of salt and cover. Cook, turning once, until lightly browned and tender, about 8 minutes total. Transfer to a plate and keep warm. Repeat with 2 more tablespoons of the oil and the remaining mushroom caps.

In the same skillet over low heat, warm the remaining 3 tablespoons olive oil. Add the garlic and red pepper, cover, and cook, stirring often without browning the garlic, for 3 minutes. Add the broccoli rabe with its clinging water, cover, and cook, stirring once or twice, until the rabe is wilted and somewhat tender, about 4 minutes.

Meanwhile, spread the cut side of the bottom *focaccia* half with the goat cheese. Set the 2 *focaccia* halves, cut side up, on a baking sheet and warm them in the oven until just heated through, about 5 minutes.

Set the *focaccia* bottom on a work surface. Spread the greens and any pan juices evenly over the goat cheese. Arrange the mushroom caps, overlapping them slightly, over the greens. Season the mushrooms generously with black pepper. Set the *focaccia* top in place. With a serrated knife, cut the sandwich into quarters. Serve warm.

Variation: Replace the goat cheese with whole-milk ricotta that has been drained in a fine-mesh strainer for 30 minutes. Other wild or exotic mushrooms can be substituted. Other greens, such as spinach or Swiss chard, can replace or join the rabe.

Pan Bagnat

makes 1 big sandwich, serving 4

This stuffed loaf is a specialty of Provence, especially Nice. The name means "bathed bread," and the generously dressed sandwich is often served to celebrate the first pressing of the olive oil. Pan bagnat is prepared an hour or two in advance--ideal picnic fare--and weighted, which allows the garlicky vinaigrette to penetrate and soften the loaf. Thus, even more than elsewhere in this book, the quality of the bread is paramount. Select a firm on the inside, slightly crusty on the outside peasant bread, preferably of sourdough. The round shape is traditional, but the sandwich can be adapted to fit any appropriate bread you find.

1	large, heavy green or red sweet pepper
4	garlic cloves, mashed
3	tablespoons red wine vinegar
½	teaspoon Dijon mustard
½	teaspoon salt
½	teaspoon freshly ground black pepper
⅔	cup olive oil
1	round loaf crusty peasant bread, about 8 inches in diameter and 3 inches thick, split horizontally
1	large, ripe tomato, cut into 6 thin slices
12	large fresh basil leaves
1	can (6⅛ ounces) oil-packed chunk light tuna, drained
1	small red onion, thinly sliced and separated into rings
6	oil-packed, caper-filled rolled anchovy fillets, drained and minced
2	cups mesclun (mixed baby salad greens)

In the open flame of a gas burner, or under a preheated broiler, roast the pepper, turning it often, until the peel is lightly and evenly charred. Slip the pepper into a paper bag, close the top, and steam the pepper until cool. Rub away the blackened peel, then stem and core the pepper and cut it into thin strips.

In a small bowl, whisk together the garlic, vinegar, mustard, salt, and pepper. Slowly whisk in the olive oil; the dressing will thicken.

Drizzle each cut side of the loaf of bread with ⅓ cup of the dressing. Arrange the tomato slices over the cut side of the bottom of the loaf, overlapping them if necessary. Arrange the basil leaves over the tomatoes. Flake the tuna over the basil. Scatter the pepper strips and onion rings over the tuna.

In a medium bowl, stir together the anchovies and the remaining dressing. Add the mesclun and toss. Pile the mesclun onto the tuna. Set the top of the loaf in place and press lightly with the palm of your hand to flatten it slightly. Wrap the sandwich in plastic, weight it (with a heavy pot lid, for example), and let it stand at room temperature for at least 1 hour or for up to 2 hours.

Unwrap the sandwich. With a serrated knife, cut it into quarters. Serve immediately.

Variation: Chopped pitted Greek black olives (about 6) can be added to the mesclun along with, or in place of, the anchovies.

Oven-Baked Eggplant Parmigiana Heroes

makes 4 big sandwiches

My memories of Brooklyn, where I lived for nearly fifteen years, include the eggplant parmigiana heroes--always spelled hero's in Brooklyn-- delivered often from Smiling Pizzeria (next to the subway stop, corner of Seventh Avenue and Ninth Street). Foil wrapped, hot, and steamy, they are napped with a tangy tomato sauce and gooey with cheese. My new hometown has many virtues, but a restaurant delivering an eggplant sandwich as good as Smiling's is not among them, hence this re-creation, which, especially here in New Mexico, tastes every bit as good as the genuine thing.

2 medium eggplants (about 1½ pounds total)
2 teaspoons salt
1 cup Italian-seasoned fine, dried bread crumbs
⅓ cup grated Parmesan cheese
3 eggs
4 tablespoons olive oil
2 loaves Italian or soft French bread, each about 14 inches long, ends trimmed, cut into four 6-inch-long sections, and split horizontally
1⅓ cups tomato sauce, homemade or purchased, heated to simmering
½ pound processed provolone cheese, thinly sliced

Trim the eggplants. Cut them in half lengthwise; cut each half crosswise into ½-inch-thick pieces. In a colander set over a plate, layer the eggplant slices, sprinkling them evenly with the salt as you go. Let stand for 1 hour. Pat the eggplant slices dry.

In a wide, shallow dish, mix together the bread crumbs and Parmesan. In a second wide, shallow dish, thoroughly whisk the eggs.

In a large, heavy skillet over medium heat, warm 2 tablespoons of the olive oil. Working in batches, dip the eggplant slices into the beaten egg, let the excess drip off, then dredge the slices in the seasoned crumbs, coating them well on all sides. Lay the coated eggplant slices in the oil and cook, turning them once or twice, until they are crisp and browned, about 4 minutes per side. Drain the browned eggplant slices on paper towels. Repeat with the remaining eggplant and the remaining 2 tablespoons oil. The eggplant can be fried up to 2 hours in advance. Reserve, covered, in a single layer, at room temperature.

Position a rack in the middle of an oven and preheat to 400 degrees F. Prepare four 8-by-10-inch pieces of heavy-duty aluminum foil. Arrange the eggplant slices, overlapping them slightly, on the bottoms of the 4 sections of bread; use all the eggplant. Nap the eggplant with the hot tomato sauce, dividing it evenly and using it all. Arrange the provolone, cutting the slices to fit as necessary, over the sauce. Set the top halves of the bread sections in place and press lightly with the palm of your hand to flatten them slightly. Wrap each sandwich in a square of foil, sealing it tightly.

Set the sandwiches directly on the oven rack and bake them until they are hot and steaming and the cheese is melted, about 20 minutes. Transfer the wrapped sandwiches to a wire rack to cool for 5 minutes. Serve, if desired, in the foil.

Russian Radish, Sour Cream, and Pumpernickel Sandwiches

makes 4 big sandwiches

I had an indelible memory of this deeply flavored yet light sandwich, as mentioned, without recipe, in Mimi Sheraton's culinary memoir, From My Mother's Kitchen. A recent rereading of the revised edition of that book revealed various pairings of all the major ingredients, but nowhere could I find mention of the united whole. Wherever it came from, then, it's a wonderful, gardeny-fresh, hot-weather sandwich that requires, because of its simplicity, impeccable ingredients. Enjoy it with a tall glass of seltzer.

1⅓ cups good-quality sour cream

2 green onions, trimmed and thinly sliced (include the tops)

About 30 very crisp red radishes, trimmed, rinsed, and well chilled

8 large, thick slices best-quality pumpernickel or black bread

Salt

Freshly ground black pepper

In a medium bowl, stir together the sour cream and green onions. Cover and refrigerate until cold.

On the slicing side of a box grater, thinly slice the radishes. Lay 4 slices of the bread on a work surface. Spread the sour cream mixture thickly over the slices, dividing it evenly and using it all. Top the sour cream with the radishes, layering them evenly to the edges of the bread and using them all. Generously season the radishes with salt and pepper to taste. Set the remaining 4 bread slices atop the radishes.

With a sharp knife, cut the sandwiches in half on the diagonal. Serve immediately.

New Waves

Pesto Chicken Sandwiches with Roasted Red Peppers and Fontina

makes 4 big sandwiches

Using convenient purchased pesto makes these colorful open-faced sandwiches fairly quick to assemble. Serve them on the same plate with a big salad of romaine, arugula, and tomatoes dressed with olive oil and balsamic vinegar (mopping up of vinaigrette with bread is encouraged), and drink an uncomplicated cold white wine such as Soave.

1	large, heavy red sweet pepper
2	boneless, skinless whole chicken breasts (about 1½ pounds total)
½	cup pesto sauce
2	tablespoons olive oil
2	tablespoons unsalted butter, at room temperature
2	garlic cloves, mashed
¼	teaspoon salt, plus salt to taste
¼	teaspoon freshly ground black pepper, plus freshly ground black pepper to taste
4	large, thick slices crusty country-style bread
½	pound Fontina Val d'Aosta cheese, rind trimmed, thinly sliced

In the flame of a gas burner or under a preheated broiler, roast the pepper, turning it, until the skin is lightly and evenly charred. Slip the pepper into a paper bag, close the top, and steam the pepper until cool. Rub away the burnt peel, them stem and core the pepper and cut it into thin strips.

Trim the chicken breasts, reserving the tenderloins for another purpose. Cut away and discard the central cartilage; there should be 4 separate chicken fillets. In a shallow bowl, combine the chicken fillets and pesto, coating the chicken evenly. Cover and marinate at room temperature for 1 hour.

In a small bowl, stir together the olive oil, butter, garlic, the ¼ teaspoon salt, and the ¼ teaspoon pepper.

Preheat a broiler. Set a large skillet over medium heat. Add the chicken fillets and cook, turning them once or twice and basting them with any pesto remaining in the bowl, until they are just cooked through and lightly browned, 6 to 8 minutes. Transfer the chicken breasts to a cutting board, tent with foil, and let stand for 5 minutes. Cut the chicken breasts into thin slices, cutting across the grain and at a slight angle. Season the sliced chicken to taste with salt and pepper.

Meanwhile, spread the bread slices on one side with the butter mixture, dividing it evenly and using it all. Lay the bread slices, buttered side up, on a broilerproof pan. Broil the bread until bubbly and lightly colored, about 3 minutes.

Remove the bread from the broiler. Arrange the chicken, overlapping the slices slightly, atop the broiled bread, dividing it evenly and using it all. Arrange the pepper strips over the chicken. Lay the Fontina slices over the pepper strips. Return the sandwiches to the broiler and cook until the cheese melts and is bubbly, about 3 minutes. Transfer the sandwiches to plates and serve immediately.

Variation: Use a large fresh poblano chile in place of the sweet pepper.

Peanut Butter, Bacon, and Pepper Jelly Sandwiches

makes 4 big sandwiches

Certain desperate midnight foragings turn out to be good enough
to plan for and repeat, which is how this odd-sounding but delicious sandwich
came to be. Washed down with a glass or two of ice-cold milk, it's now
a frequent quick and comforting supper at my house. For the best balance
of flavors, use the hottest pepper jelly you can find.

12   strips thick-cut bacon (about 1 pound total)
8   slices of firm, white sandwich bread, toasted
¾   cup peanut butter, smooth or chunky
½   cup hot pepper jelly

Lay the bacon strips in a large skillet. Set the skillet over medium heat and cook, turning the bacon once or twice, until the strips are crisp, about 8 minutes. Drain on paper towels.

Divide the peanut butter evenly among 4 slices of the bread, spreading it to the edges of the slices and using it all. Spread the pepper jelly over the peanut butter, dividing it evenly and using it all. Lay the bacon strips over the pepper jelly. Set the remaining slices of toast atop the bacon. With a sharp knife, cut the sandwiches in half on the diagonal. Serve immediately.

Ham and Brie Sandwiches with Honey Mustard
makes 4 big sandwiches

Sandwich perfection can be elusive, even unknowable. Cut the meat too thick (or too thin), forget to bring the cheese to room temperature, use too little mayo or too much, spread the ingredients over a larger than ideal square inchage of bread, and something fine becomes something ordinary. When the ingredient list is short, failure always lurks. Case in point, this combination, perfected at an Upper East Side Manhattan cheese shop, La Fromagerie, and worth trying at home until you, too, get it right.

2	thick, crusty loaves French bread (*batards*), each about 14 inches long, ends trimmed, cut into four 6-inch-long sections, and partially split horizontally
½	cup hot honey mustard
¾	pound smoky baked ham, thickly sliced
½	pound imported Brie cheese, rind intact, thickly sliced and at room temperature

Evenly spread the cut sides of the bread sections with the honey mustard, using it all. Arrange the ham slices over the mustard on the bottoms of the sandwiches, dividing them evenly. Arrange the Brie over the ham, dividing it evenly and using it all. Close the sandwiches and press them firmly with the palm of your hand to flatten slightly.

With a serrated knife, cut each sandwich in half on the diagonal. Serve immediately.

Variation: Replace the hot honey mustard with Dijon mustard; replace the Brie with thinly sliced Gruyère cheese.

Roast Fillet of Beef and Caviar Sandwiches
makes 8 big sandwiches

A definite splurge, the ultimate surf-and-turf, these elegantly primitive sandwiches should be served to your nearest and dearest at some special, but laid-back event--New Year's Eve, perhaps, spent sensibly and snugly at home in front of a crackling fire instead of coping with the unruly masses outdoors. Sadly, made with anything less than prime fillet and premium caviar, these are dull, ordinary, and not worth the calories. Drink--you guessed it-- best-quality, not too dry Champagne.

1   center-cut prime fillet of beef (chateaubriand), about 2½ pounds, tied
1   tablespoon olive oil
¼   teaspoon salt, plus salt to taste
¼   teaspoon freshly ground black pepper, plus freshly ground black pepper to taste
16 slices firm white or whole-wheat sandwich bread
8   ounces Russian beluga or osetra caviar

Bring the fillet of beef to room temperature. Position a rack in the middle of an oven and preheat to 500 degrees F. Set the fillet on a rack in a shallow roasting pan. Rub the meat with the olive oil; sprinkle it evenly with the ¼ teaspoon salt and the ¼ teaspoon pepper.

Set the fillet in the oven. Immediately lower the temperature to 250 degrees F. Roast the meat until an instant-read thermometer inserted into the thickest part registers 140 degrees F, about 1 hour. The outside of the roast will be well browned and the inside evenly rare from center to edge. Transfer the roast to a cutting board and let cool to room temperature.

Remove the strings from the fillet. Carve the meat, across the grain and at a slight angle, into thin slices. Lay 8 slices of bread on a work surface. Arrange the meat over the slices, dividing it evenly and using it all. Season the meat lightly with salt (good caviar is not salty) and generously with pepper (pepper complements caviar wonderfully). Spread the caviar over the beef, dividing it evenly and using it all.

Set the remaining slices of bread atop the caviar and press lightly with the palm of your hand to flatten them slightly. With a serrated knife, cut the sandwiches in half on the diagonal. Serve immediately.

Stilton Burgers with Red Onion Jam

makes 4 big sandwiches

The extraordinary English cheese, Stilton, combining as it does flavors of both Cheddar and blue cheeses, makes a compelling accompaniment to beef of any kind. Here, a kind of Stilton dressing tops hot, juicy burgers, while a slow-cooked jamlike relish of red onions provides a sweetly savory contrast. If you find no Stilton, spread the buns with a premium (chunky) bottled blue-cheese salad dressing into which you have stirred some grated sharp Cheddar.

10	ounces Stilton cheese
⅓	cup mayonnaise, fresh (page 89) or purchased
½	teaspoon freshly ground black pepper
2	tablespoons corn oil
2	medium-sized red onions (about ¾ pound total), thinly sliced
2	teaspoons Worcestershire sauce
½	teaspoon soy sauce
½	teaspoon packed brown sugar
1½	pounds ground beef
4	Nice Buns (page 87) or any large, round good-quality hamburger buns, split horizontally

Trim any hard rind from the cheese. In a small bowl mash together the cheese and mayonnaise until well mixed. Stir in the pepper.

In a large, heavy nonstick skillet over medium heat, warm the corn oil. Add the onions, cover, and cook, stirring occasionally, until tender and golden, about 15 minutes. Stir in the Worcestershire sauce, soy sauce, and sugar, and cook uncovered, stirring often, until the onions are well browned, about 5 minutes. The cheese mixture and the onions can be prepared up to 1 day ahead. Cover and store separately in the refrigerator; return both to room temperature before proceeding.

Preheat a broiler. Form the ground beef into 4 thick patties. Set a large, heavy skillet, preferably nonstick, over medium heat. Add the patties and cook until crisp and brown on the first side, about 5 minutes. Turn the patties and top them with the onion mixture, dividing it evenly and using it all. Cover the skillet and cook until the patties are crisp and brown on the second side and done to your liking, and the onion mixture is heated through, about 4 minutes for medium-rare beef.

Meanwhile, under the broiler, lightly toast the cut sides of the buns. Spread the tops of the buns with the Stilton mixture, dividing it evenly and using it all. Set the bottoms of the buns on plates. Place the patties on the bottoms, set the tops in place, and serve immediately.

Variation: Top each burger with a slice of tomato, a leaf of crisp lettuce, or both.

Shropshire Duck

This meatless sandwich is named in the same ironic spirit as Welsh rabbit,
I believe, and was first served to me by its creator, who insisted only
whole-wheat onion bread, prepared with his century-old Scottish sourdough starter,
would do. Shalom and his starter are gone, but I have provided a
yeast-risen version of the bread for the adventurous, and I encourage you to
give it a try. The browned onions add some ineffable quality that makes
this extraordinary eating.

8   large, thick slices whole-wheat bread,
    preferably Whole-wheat Red Onion Bread
    (page 85)
¾   pound good-quality sharp Cheddar cheese,
    thickly sliced, at room temperature
1   cup good-quality raspberry jam

Lay 4 of the bread slices on a work surface. Arrange the cheese slices, overlapping them if necessary, over the bread, dividing them evenly and using them all. Spread the raspberry jam over the cheese, dividing it evenly and using it all. Set the 4 remaining bread slices atop the jam.

Press the sandwiches lightly with the palm of your hand to flatten them slightly. With a sharp knife, cut each sandwich in half on the diagonal. Serve immediately.

Smoked Turkey and Gruyère Sandwiches on Orange Date Bread

makes 4 big sandwiches

Exotic flavors mark this sandwich combination, but none overwhelm, and together a very satisfying harmony is created. The fine-textured, not-too-sweet bread is particularly satisfying to bake and to eat, but to save kitchen time, you can substitute purchased raisin bread and stir 2 teaspoons minced orange zest into the green peppercorn butter.

8   large, angle-cut slices Orange Date Bread (page 86)
Green Peppercorn Butter (page 91), at room temperature
1   pound smoked turkey, thinly sliced
½   pound Gruyère cheese, rind trimmed and thickly sliced, at room temperature

Up to 30 minutes before serving time, lay the bread slices on a work surface. Spread 1 side of each bread slice with some of the green peppercorn butter, dividing it evenly and using it all. Ruffle the turkey slices onto 4 slices of the bread, dividing them evenly. Arrange the cheese slices over the turkey, dividing them evenly. Invert the remaining 4 bread slices, buttered side down, onto the cheese.

Press the sandwiches lightly with the palm of your hand to flatten them slightly. With a serrated knife, cut the sandwiches in half on the diagonal. Cover them with plastic wrap and drape with a dampened towel until serving.

No Recipe Required

Years ago, someone (who should have known better) asked me why I wrote chile recipes: "Don't you just make it up as you go along, mostly out of leftovers?" Well, no, I don't, not chile anyway, and not sandwiches, usually, either, except sometimes, yes, I do. For order in the kitchen as well as accuracy of reproduction, this book does contain actual sandwich recipes, but recognizing that some of the best sandwiches require a more improvisational spirit (not to mention a pantry, a refrigerator, and a bread box at least reasonably stocked with ingredients of wildly varying potential), I offer the following by way of aid to memory, call to muse, and general encouragement. The rest is up to you.

Thickly sliced country pâté, Dijon mustard, and cornichons on baguette

Hot dog, chili con carne, grated Cheddar cheese, pickled jalapeño slices, and chopped yellow onion on a toasted hot dog roll

Knockwurst, sauerkraut, Swiss cheese, and grainy beer mustard on a hot dog roll

Hot sliced beef brisket and brown gravy, served open-faced on white sandwich bread

Hot sliced turkey, stuffing, and gravy, served open-faced on white sandwich bread; add cranberry sauce if desired

Griddled burger with melted cheese, mayonnaise or Russian dressing, tomato, lettuce, and onion on toasted hamburger bun

Mustardy egg salad, tomato, and lettuce on toasted white or whole-wheat sandwich bread

Warm sliced meat loaf and ketchup or Russian dressing on crusty white bread; include sliced tomato, crisp lettuce, or both

Sliced hot pastrami with spicy brown mustard on rye bread

Sliced hot corned beef with Dijon mustard and Swiss cheese on a hard roll

American cheese griddled on well-buttered white sandwich bread; include sliced tomato, crisp bacon, or both

Peanut butter (preferably chunky) and jelly (preferably Concord grape) on white bread

Chopped chicken liver on rye bread

Tuna salad and American cheese on white sandwich bread, broiled until the cheese is bubbly and lightly browned

Cream cheese and jelly on toasted white sandwich bread

Sliced beefsteak tomatoes and mayonnaise from a jar on white sandwich bread; eat bending over the kitchen sink

Fried egg, melted American cheese, and sliced tomato on whole-wheat toast

Sliced ham, Swiss cheese, honey mustard, sliced tomato, and lettuce on white sandwich bread

Apple butter, peanut butter, and sweet butter on nutted whole-grain bread

Liverwurst or braunschweiger, thinly sliced red onion, and spicy brown mustard on pumpernickel bread

Thinly sliced salami, provolone, and sliced hot cherry peppers on semolina bread

Hummus, tomato chunks, onion chunks, and cucumber chunks in whole-wheat pita bread

Leftover meatballs, leftover tomato sauce, and mozzarella cheese on semolina bread; wrap in foil and bake until bubbly

Leftover sliced steak, blue-cheese dressing, tomatoes, and lettuce on crusty country-style bread

Leftover sliced steak, horseradish, mayonnaise, and crisp lettuce on toasted white sandwich bread

Leftover sliced roast leg of lamb, *tapenade*, sliced yellow tomatoes, and fresh basil leaves on baguette

Leftover roast chicken, garlic mayonnaise, and fresh spinach on walnut bread

Leftover baked beans and crisp bacon on Boston brown bread or any whole-grain bread

Crisp patties of corned beef hash topped with a fried egg on a toasted kaiser roll; serve with warmed ketchup

Leftover barbecued chicken, shredded, moistened with extra sauce, and then piled on a bun; top with grated jalapeño Jack cheese and broil until bubbly

Sardines, unsalted butter and/or Dijon mustard, and thinly sliced red onion on rye or pumpernickel bread

Egg salad, smoked salmon, and thinly sliced red onion on seeded rye bread

Leftover roast pork, sautéed mushrooms, and tarragon mustard on raisin pumpernickel bread

Leftover grilled vegetables and *baba ghannouj* (eggplant and sesame purée) on toasted *focaccia*

Leftover ratatouille and fresh goat or sheep cheese on oil-brushed, griddled semolina bread

Peppery French-Toasted Ham-and-Apple-Butter Sandwiches

makes 2 big sandwiches

Somewhat less than batter-crisped Monte Cristos, but far more than plain French toast, these eggy, double-decker, ham-and-apple sandwiches make a wonderful brunch or cozy supper. Since there's a certain amount of dexterity involved in getting the sandwiches out of the soaking mixture and into a skillet, the recipe is written for two. Those with several large skillets (or a professional range with a built-in griddle) and a certain amount of practice time in, however, should be able to turn these out for a crowd. The sandwiches are best if served straight from the fat, not held in the oven.

4	eggs
1	cup milk
1	teaspoon freshly ground black pepper
¼	teaspoon salt
6	slices day-old firm white sandwich bread
½	pound best-quality, smoky baked ham, thinly sliced
¼	cup natural, unsweetened apple butter
½	stick (4 tablespoons) unsalted butter
	Warmed maple syrup for serving

In a shallow dish, thoroughly whisk the eggs. Whisk in the milk, pepper and salt.

Lay 2 slices of the bread on a work surface. Top each with one-fourth of the ham. Spread 1 tablespoon of the apple butter on one side of each of 2 more slices of bread. Invert the bread slices, apple butter down, onto the ham. Spread the remaining apple butter on the now-upward side of the bread slices. Top the apple butter with the remaining ham, dividing it evenly. Set the remaining bread slices atop the ham. With a serrated knife, carefully cut the sandwiches in half on the diagonal.

In a large skillet over medium heat, melt the butter. Meanwhile, working in batches, set the sandwich halves in the egg mixture, let them sit briefly, and then, with a large spatula, carefully turn them over. Baste the halves with some of the egg mixture, then carefully transfer them to a plate.

When the butter is foaming, carefully add the sandwich halves to the skillet. Cook until crisp and golden on the first side, about 3 minutes. With a large spatula, carefully turn the sandwich halves and cook until crisp and golden on the second side, another 3 minutes.

Carefully transfer the sandwich halves to plates and serve immediately, passing maple syrup at the table.

Curried Turkey Meatball Sandwiches with Cranberry Raita

makes 4 big sandwiches

Jalapeño, ginger, garlic, and curry powder all add a little fiery excitement
to otherwise rather uninteresting supermarket ground turkey.
Served stuffed into chunks of good bread (pitas can be substituted) and
napped with a sweetly cooling yogurt relish, or raita, the crusty meatballs make
a lively and unusual sandwich.

¾ cup corn oil
1 fresh jalapeño chile, stemmed and minced
2 teaspoons curry powder
1 garlic clove, minced
1½ teaspoons grated fresh ginger
1 pound ground turkey
1 egg, beaten
3 tablespoons unseasoned fine dried
  bread crumbs
½ teaspoon salt
½ plain yogurt
½ cup whole-berry cranberry sauce, chilled
2 tablespoons finely chopped fresh cilantro
2 loaves crusty Italian bread, each about
  14 inches long, ends trimmed, cut into four
  6-inch-long sections, and split horizontally

In a small, heavy skillet over low heat warm 1½ tablespoons of the corn oil. Add the jalapeño, curry powder, garlic, and ginger, and cook, stirring often without browning, for 10 minutes. Let cool slightly.

In a medium bowl combine the turkey, egg, jalapeño mixture, bread crumbs, and salt, and stir just until combined. Form the meat mixture into 12 equal balls. Set the meatballs on a plate, cover, and refrigerate for 1 hour.

In a small bowl, mix together the yogurt, cranberry sauce, and cilantro.

In a large, heavy skillet over medium heat, warm the remaining corn oil. Add the meatballs and cook, turning occasionally, until well browned on all sides and just cooked through while remaining juicy, about 10 minutes. With a slotted spoon, transfer the meatballs to paper towels to drain briefly.

Fill each bread section with 3 meatballs. Generously top the meatballs with some of the yogurt mixture, dividing it evenly and using it all. Serve immediately.

Variation: Finely ground lean lamb can be substituted for the turkey. Mango chutney can be substituted for the cranberry sauce.

Corned Beef Sandwiches with Tangy Beet Slaw

makes 4 big sandwiches

Corned beef, tasted for the first time at its best in a quintessential New York delicatessen, captured me completely (and affirmed what I already knew from the family tree, that my gene pool formed somewhere in the British Isles). The sweetly mustardy beet slaw is my own contribution to the large and traditional genre of corned beef garnishes-relishes, all designed to counterbalance the slightly salty meat. (Corned beef from a can, as well as processed sandwich slices, are unsuitable for this recipe, although prepared, sliced meat, purchased from a good deli, is an excellent timesaver.) The beets are baked in the oven, producing a deeper, sweeter flavor.

1	corned brisket of beef, about 3 pounds
2	medium-large beets (about 1 pound total)
1	small red cabbage (about 1 pound)
1	cup mayonnaise, fresh (page 89) or purchased
2	tablespoons fresh lemon juice
2	tablespoons sugar
2	tablespoons coarse-grain mustard
8	large slices pumpernickel or seeded-rye bread, each ½ inch thick

In a 4- to 5-quart dutch oven, place the corned beef, fat side up. Add water to come halfway up the sides of the beef. If a spice packet was included with the beef, open it and stir the spices into the water. Set over medium heat and bring to a simmer. Cover partially, reduce the heat to low, and cook gently until the beef is very tender, 2½ to 3 hours. Let the beef rest in the water for 10 minutes, then transfer it to a cutting board. Remove and discard the fat. Carve the meat into thin slices, cutting across the grain and at a slight angle. The beef can be used immediately, or it can be cooled to room temperature. Wrap tightly in foil and refrigerate for up to 2 days; rewarm the beef in the foil in a preheated 300 degree F oven until steaming, about 20 minutes, before proceeding.

Meanwhile, position a rack in the middle of the oven and preheat to 400 degrees F. Trim off the beet tops, leaving about ½ inch of stem. Wrap the beets in foil and bake for about 1 hour, or until very tender. Remove from the oven and let cool to room temperature in the foil. Unwrap the beets and peel them. The beets can be prepared up to 2 days in advance. Wrap them well and refrigerate; return them to room temperature before proceeding.

Trim, quarter, and core the cabbage and, using a long, sharp knife, cut it into julienne. Grate the beets coarsely. In a medium bowl, whisk together the mayonnaise, lemon juice, sugar, and mustard. Add the cabbage and beets and stir to combine.

Lay 4 slices of bread on a work surface. Top with hot corned beef, dividing it evenly and using it all. Top the corned beef with the beet slaw, dividing it evenly and using it all. Set the remaining 4 slices of bread atop the slaw. With a serrated knife, carefully cut the sandwiches in half on the diagonal. Serve immediately.

Breads and Spreads

Whole-Wheat Red Onion Bread

Orange Date Bread

Nice Buns

Whole-Wheat Toasted-Cornmeal Bread

Fresh Mayonnaise

Green Chile Mayonnaise

Tabasco Toasted-Pecan Mayonnaise

Creole Dressing

Green Peppercorn Butter

Whole-Wheat Red Onion Bread

makes 1 big loaf

This grainy, oniony bread is particularly good in cheese sandwiches or with tuna salad. I like a big, freeform oval bread (with correspondingly odd-shaped slices) but the dough can also be halved and baked in two 9-by-5-inch loaf pans.

2   cups warm (105 to 115 degrees F) water
2   tablespoons molasses
1   package (¼ ounce) active dry yeast
3   cups stone-ground whole-wheat flour
1   tablespoon salt
    About 2 cups unbleached all-purpose flour
3   tablespoons corn oil
2   medium-sized red onions (about ¾ pound total), thinly sliced
1   teaspoon sugar
1   teaspoon soy sauce
2   tablespoons yellow cornmeal

In a large bowl, stir together the water and molasses. Whisk in the yeast and let stand until foamy, about 5 minutes. One cup at a time, whisk in the whole-wheat flour. Stir in about 1 cup of the white flour until a sticky but manageable dough forms. Flour a work surface heavily with some of the remaining white flour. Turn out the dough and knead, incorporating additional white flour as required to form a dough that is satiny and smooth, about 5 minutes.

Shape the dough into a ball. In a large bowl, turn the ball of dough in 1 tablespoon of the corn oil until evenly coated. Cover the bowl with a kitchen towel and let rise in a draft-free spot until doubled in bulk, about 1½ hours.

Punch down the dough, turn it out onto a lightly floured work surface, and knead for 3 minutes. Re-form it into a ball, return it to the bowl, cover the bowl with the towel, and let stand in a draft-free spot until the dough is doubled in bulk, about 1 hour.

Meanwhile, in a large, heavy skillet, preferably nonstick, over medium-low heat, warm the remaining 2 tablespoons corn oil. Stir in the onions, sugar, and soy sauce and cook uncovered, stirring occasionally, until lightly browned, about 8 minutes. Let cool to room temperature.

Dust a large, heavy baking sheet with the cornmeal. Punch down the dough. Turn it out onto a lightly floured work surface and form it into an oval loaf about 14 inches long. Transfer the loaf to the prepared baking sheet, cover with the towel, and let rise for 30 minutes.

Position a rack in the middle of an oven and preheat to 400 degrees F.

Set the baking sheet on the rack and bake the bread for 15 minutes. Spoon the onions and any oil from the skillet evenly over the top of the loaf and continue to bake until the crust is crisp, the onions are well browned but not burned, and the loaf sounds hollow when the bottom is thumped, about 25 minutes.

Transfer the loaf to a wire rack and let cool to room temperature before slicing.

Orange Date Bread

makes one 9-by-5-inch loaf

This bread, adapted from a recipe by James Beard, is delicious with curried tuna salad (page 40) or toasted and served for breakfast with a little butter and honey.

1 cup fresh orange juice
¼ cup plus 1 tablespoon water
3 tablespoons unsalted butter, plus unsalted butter at room temperature for the pan
3 tablespoons minced orange zest (orange peel)
2 tablespoons honey
2 teaspoons salt
2 teaspoons active dry yeast
About 3½ cups unbleached all-purpose flour
1 tablespoon corn oil
¾ cup coarsely chopped pitted dates
1 egg

In a small, nonreactive saucepan over low heat, combine the orange juice, the ¼ cup water, the 3 tablespoons butter, the orange zest, honey, and salt. Heat, stirring, just until the butter melts.

Pour the orange juice mixture into a large bowl and let cool to between 105 and 115 degrees F. Stir in the yeast and let stand until foamy, about 5 minutes. One cup at a time, whisk in 2½ cups of the flour until a sticky but manageable dough forms. Flour a work surface heavily with some of the remaining flour. Turn out the dough and knead, incorporating additional flour as required to make a dough that is satiny and smooth, about 5 minutes.

Shape the dough into a ball. In a large bowl, turn the ball of dough in the corn oil until evenly coated.

Cover the bowl with a kitchen towel and let rise in a draft-free spot until doubled in bulk, about 1½ hours.

Punch down the dough, turn it out onto a lightly floured work surface, and knead for 3 minutes. Re-form it into a ball, return it to the bowl, cover the bowl with the towel, and let stand in a draft-free spot until the dough is doubled in bulk, about 1 hour.

Butter a 9-by-5-by-3-inch loaf pan. Turn out the dough onto a lightly floured work surface and flatten it. Scatter the chopped dates evenly over the dough. Gather the dough into a ball and knead it briefly to distribute the dates evenly throughout the dough. Form the dough into a loaf shape and transfer the dough to the prepared pan. Cover the pan with the towel and let stand in a draft-free spot until the dough has risen level with the rim of the pan.

Meanwhile, position a rack in the middle of an oven and preheat to 400 degrees F.

In a small bowl, whisk together the egg and the 1 table-spoon water. Using a pastry brush, glaze the top of the loaf with the egg mixture (you will not need it all). Set the pan on the oven rack and bake for 20 minutes. Reduce the heat to 350 degrees F and bake until the loaf has risen, is well browned, and sounds hollow when the bottom is thumped, about 20 more minutes.

Transfer the loaf to a wire rack and let cool completely. Wrap well and store at room temperature for 1 day before slicing.

Nice Buns
makes 8 large buns

Good buns are rarer than good burgers, bad buns being so much a part of the burger experience by now that only the fussiest of us can separate the fair from the fine. The odd bakery still takes pride in a burger bun that is not all sweeteners, conditioners, and air, but they are scarce indeed. My new town has just such a bakery, but before I lived here I was compelled to bake up my own, from the formula below. If you are fewer than eight, and not gluttonous, extras freeze beautifully.

1½ cups milk
1   cup plus 1 tablespoon water
½   stick (4 tablespoons) unsalted butter, plus unsalted butter at room temperature for the baking sheet
1   tablespoon sugar
1   tablespoon salt
1   package (¼ ounce) active dry yeast
    About 5 cups unbleached all-purpose flour
1   tablespoon corn oil
1   egg
2   teaspoons sesame, poppy, caraway, fennel, or cumin seeds (optional)

In a small saucepan over low heat, combine the milk, the 1 cup water, the ½ stick butter, sugar, and salt. Set over low heat and warm, stirring, until the butter just melts. Transfer the milk mixture to a large mixing bowl and let cool to between 105 and 115 degrees F.

Whisk the yeast into the milk mixture and let stand until foamy, about 5 minutes. Gradually stir in about 4 cups of the flour until a sticky but manageable dough forms. Turn out the dough onto a floured work surface and knead, incorporating additional flour as required to make a dough that is smooth and elastic, about 5 minutes.

Shape the dough into a ball. In a large mixing bowl, turn the dough in the corn oil to coat. Cover the bowl with a kitchen towel and let the dough rise in a draft-free spot until doubled in bulk, about 1½ hours.

Butter a baking sheet. Punch down the dough, then turn it out onto a lightly floured work surface. Divide the dough into 8 equal pieces. Shape each piece into a ball and transfer to the prepared sheet, spacing the balls about 2 inches apart. Cover the baking sheet with the towel and let rise until doubled in bulk, about 30 minutes.

Meanwhile, position a rack in the middle of an oven and preheat to 450 degrees F.

In a small bowl, whisk together the egg and the 1 tablespoon water. Using a pastry brush, glaze the tops of the buns with the egg mixture. Sprinkle the seeds evenly over the buns. Set the baking sheet on the oven rack and reduce the temperature to 400 degrees F. Bake until the buns are puffed, crisp, and lightly browned, 25 to 30 minutes.

Transfer the buns to a wire rack and let cool completely. The buns can be used immediately (although they will be easier to slice if they are 1 day old; wrap airtight and store at room temperature). The buns can also be frozen for up to 2 months.

Whole-Wheat Toasted-Cornmeal Bread

makes one 9-by-5-inch loaf

Toasting the cornmeal adds crunch and a subtle, nutty flavor.
Although slow to rise, this loaf keeps well, at room temperature or frozen, and
makes wonderful sandwiches and excellent toast.

½   cup yellow cornmeal, preferably stone-ground
1½   cups warm (105 to 115 degrees F) water
1   tablespoon honey
1   package (¼ ounce) active dry yeast
3   tablespoons corn oil, plus corn oil for the
      baking pan
1½   teaspoons salt
1   cup whole-wheat flour,
      preferably stone-ground
2–2½ cups unbleached all-purpose flour

Position a rack in the middle of an oven and preheat to 400 degrees F. Spread the cornmeal in a shallow metal pan (a cake tin would be good) and bake, stirring occasionally, until fragrant and lightly browned, 15 to 20 minutes. Remove from the oven and let cool to room temperature.

In a large mixing bowl, whisk together the water and honey. Whisk in the yeast and let stand until foamy, about 5 minutes.

Stir in the cornmeal, 2 tablespoons of the corn oil, and the salt. Stir in the whole-wheat flour and about 1½ cups of the white flour until a sticky dough forms. Turn out the dough onto a well-floured work surface and

knead, incorporating additional white flour as required to form a fairly smooth dough (it will remain slightly sticky), about 5 minutes.

Shape the dough into a ball. In a large mixing bowl, turn the ball of dough in the remaining 1 tablespoon corn oil to coat. Cover the bowl with a kitchen towel. Let the dough rise in a draft-free spot until doubled in bulk, about 2 hours.

Punch down the dough and turn it out onto a lightly floured work surface. Knead for 1 minute. Re-form the dough into a ball, then return it to the bowl. Cover the bowl with the towel and let the dough rise until doubled in bulk, about 2 hours.

Lightly oil a 9-by-5-by-3-inch loaf pan. Punch down the dough and turn it out onto a lightly floured work surface. Form it into a loaf. Transfer the dough to the pan, cover with the towel, and let rise until the dough is level with the pan rim, about 1 hour.

Position a rack in the middle of an oven and preheat to 400 degrees F.

Set the pan on the rack and bake the bread for 30 minutes. Turn the bread out of the pan and set it right side up directly on the oven rack. Bake until the crust is crisp and the loaf sounds hollow when thumped on the bottom, about 5 more minutes. Transfer to a wire rack and let cool completely before cutting.

Fresh Mayonnaise

makes about 1 cup

Made with corn oil, this light, fresh mayonnaise is compatible with a wide
assortment of sandwich fillings. When prepared partly or entirely
with good olive oil, it is heavier, more aggressive and more Mediterranean.
For many sandwiches, mayo from the jar does just fine. For other sandwiches, and
other sandwich makers, only this will do.

2   egg yolks, at room temperature
2   teaspoons fresh lemon juice
1   teaspoon Dijon mustard
½   teaspoon salt, plus salt to taste
¾   cup corn or olive oil, or a mixture of the two
½   teaspoon freshly ground black pepper

In a small bowl, whisk together thoroughly the egg yolks, 1 teaspoon of the lemon juice, the mustard, and ½ teaspoon of the salt. Slowly, by drops at first, begin whisking the oil into the egg mixture. The mayonnaise will thicken. Continue to whisk; the last ¼ cup or so of oil can be added in a slow, steady stream. Whisk in the pepper and the remaining lemon juice. Season with additional salt to taste.

The mayonnaise can be prepared up to 3 days ahead. Cover and refrigerate; return it just to room temperature before using.

Variation: For Lemony Mayonnaise, stir 1 teaspoon minced lemon zest (yellow peel) and 1 additional teaspoon fresh lemon juice into the finished mayonnaise.

Green Chile Mayonnaise

makes about 1¼ cups

I'm fortunate enough to be able to buy roasted and chopped, frozen hot green chiles where I live, which is a timesaver when I want this fiery condiment in a hurry. During green chile season, though, there's nothing like the fresh thing--the mayo is immeasurably better. Try it on burgers (especially of turkey) or as a dip for grilled shrimp.

4   fresh Anaheim or other medium-hot long, green chiles, or ⅔ cup roasted and chopped, frozen hot green chiles, thawed and well drained
½   cup mayonnaise, fresh (page 89) or purchased
2   teaspoons fresh lime juice

If using fresh chiles, in the open flame of a gas burner or under a preheated broiler, roast the chiles, turning them, until they are evenly and lightly charred. Slip the chiles into a paper bag, close the top, and let steam until cool. Rub away the burnt peel, then stem and seed the chiles and chop finely. If using thawed, frozen chiles, pat dry with paper towels.

In a medium bowl, stir together the chopped chiles, mayonnaise and lime juice. The mayonnaise can be prepared up to 3 days ahead. Cover and refrigerate until using.

Tabasco Toasted-Pecan Mayonnaise

makes about 1 cup

This mayonnaise is also good on grilled or poached fish or chicken, in a sandwich or otherwise.

½   cup (about 2 ounces) pecans
1   teaspoon Tabasco sauce
1   cup mayonnaise, fresh (page 89) or purchased

Position a rack in the middle of an oven and preheat to 375 degrees F. Spread the pecans in a shallow metal pan (a pie tin works well) and toast, stirring once or twice, until crisp, fragrant, and lightly browned, 8 to 10 minutes. Remove the pecans from the pan, let cool to room temperature, and then chop them.

Just before serving, stir the pecans and Tabasco into the mayonnaise.

Creole Dressing

makes about ⅔ cup

Use a mild but flavorful hot pepper sauce, such as
Trappey's Red Devil, for best results.

1   teaspoon minced fresh thyme
¼   teaspoon salt
½   cup mayonnaise, fresh (page 89) or
     purchased
2   tablespoons minced, oil-packed sun-dried
     tomatoes
2   teaspoons hot pepper sauce
1   teaspoon Worcestershire sauce
1   teaspoon fresh lemon juice
½   teaspoon spicy brown mustard

In a medium bowl, combine the thyme and salt and, with
the back of a spoon, mash them into a rough paste. Stir in
the mayonnaise, sun-dried tomatoes, hot pepper sauce,
Worcestershire sauce, lemon juice, and mustard. Taste
and adjust the seasoning (the dressing should be spicy).

The dressing can be prepared up to 1 day ahead. Cover
and refrigerate; return it to room temperature before using.

Green Peppercorn Butter

makes about ½ cup

In addition to the turkey sandwiches on page 75, this pungent butter is good on
roast beef or roast lamb sandwiches, or melting atop a just-grilled burger.

1   tablespoon drained brine-packed green
     peppercorns
1   stick (¼ pound) unsalted butter, at room
     temperature
     Pinch of salt

In a small bowl, with the back of a spoon, mash the
green peppercorns. Add the butter and salt and combine
thoroughly. Cover and refrigerate for up to 3 days or
freeze for up to 1 month. Soften the butter to room
temperature before using.

Table of Equivalents

The exact equivalents in the following tables have been rounded for convenience.

Oven Temperatures

Fahrenheit	Celsius	Gas
250	120	½
275	140	1
300	150	2
325	160	3
350	180	4
375	190	5
400	200	6
425	220	7
450	230	8
475	240	9
500	260	10

Liquids

US	Metric	UK
2 tbl	30 ml	1 fl oz
¼ cup	60 ml	2 fl oz
⅓ cup	80 ml	3 fl oz
½ cup	125 ml	4 fl oz
⅔ cup	160 ml	5 fl oz
¾ cup	180 ml	6 fl oz
1 cup	250 ml	8 fl oz
1½ cups	375 ml	12 fl oz
2 cups	500 ml	16 fl oz
4 cups/1 qt	1 l	32 fl oz

US/UK
oz=ounce
lb=pound
in=inch
ft=foot
tbl=tablespoon
fl oz=fluid ounce
qt=quart

Metric
g=gram
kg=kilogram
mm=millimeter
cm=centimeter
ml=milliliter
l=liter

Weights

US/UK	Metric
1 oz	30 g
2 oz	60 g
3 oz	90 g
4 oz (¼ lb)	125 g
5 oz (⅓ lb)	155 g
6 oz	185 g
7 oz	220 g
8 oz (½ lb)	250 g
10 oz	315 g
12 oz (¾ lb)	375 g
14 oz	440 g
16 oz (1 lb)	500 g
1½ lb	750 g
2 lb	1 kg
3 lb	1.5 kg

Length Measures

⅛ in	3 mm
¼ in	6 mm
½ in	12 mm
1 in	2.5 cm
2 in	5 cm
3 in	7.5 cm
4 in	10 cm
5 in	13 cm
6 in	15 cm
7 in	18 cm
8 in	20 cm
9 in	23 cm
10 in	25 cm
11 in	28 cm
12 in/1 ft	30 cm

Equivalents for Commonly Used Ingredients

All-Purpose (Plain) Flour/Dried Bread Crumbs/ Chopped Nuts

¼ cup	1 oz	30 g
⅓ cup	1½ oz	45 g
½ cup	2 oz	60 g
¾ cup	3 oz	90 g
1 cup	4 oz	125 g
1½ cups	6 oz	185 g
2 cups	8 oz	250 g

Whole-Wheat (Wholemeal) Flour

3 tbl	1 oz	30 g
½ cup	2 oz	60 g
⅔ cup	3 oz	90 g
1 cup	4 oz	125 g
1¼ cups	5 oz	155 g
1⅔ cups	7 oz	210 g
1¾ cups	8 oz	250 g

Brown Sugar

¼ cup	1½ oz	45 g
½ cup	3 oz	90 g
¾ cup	4 oz	125 g
1 cup	5½ oz	170 g
1½ cups	8 oz	250 g
2 cups	10 oz	315 g

White Sugar

¼ cup	2 oz	60 g
⅓ cup	3 oz	90 g
½ cup	4 oz	125 g
¾ cup	6 oz	185 g
1 cup	8 oz	250 g
1½ cups	12 oz	375 g
2 cups	1 lb	500 g

Raisins/Currants/Semolina

¼ cup	1 oz	30 g
⅓ cup	2 oz	60 g
½ cup	3 oz	90 g
¾ cup	4 oz	125 g
1 cup	5 oz	155 g

Long-Grain Rice/Cornmeal

⅓ cup	2 oz	60 g
½ cup	2½ oz	75 g
¾ cup	4 oz	125 g
1 cup	5 oz	155 g
1½ cups	8 oz	250 g

Dried Beans

¼ cup	1½ oz	45 g
⅓ cup	2 oz	60 g
½ cup	3 oz	90 g
¾ cup	5 oz	155 g
1 cup	6 oz	185 g
1¼ cups	8 oz	250 g
1½ cups	12 oz	375 g

Rolled Oats

⅓ cup	1 oz	30 g
⅔ cup	2 oz	60 g
1 cup	3 oz	90 g
1½ cups	4 oz	125 g
2 cups	5 oz	155 g

Jam/Honey

2 tbl	2 oz	60 g
¼ cup	3 oz	90 g
½ cup	5 oz	155 g
¾ cup	8 oz	250 g
1 cup	11 oz	345 g

Grated Parmesan/ Romano Cheese

¼ cup	1 oz	30 g
½ cup	2 oz	60 g
¾ cup	3 oz	90 g
1 cup	4 oz	125 g
1⅓ cups	5 oz	155 g
2 cups	7 oz	220 g